SUN-RISE

SUN-RISE

Addresses from a City Pulpit

BY THE

REV. G. H. MORRISON, M.A.

BAKER BOOK HOUSE
Grand Rapids, Michigan

Reprinted 1971 by
Baker Book House Company

ISBN: 0-8010-5889-9

PHOTOLITHOPRINTED BY CUSHING - MALLOY, INC.
ANN ARBOR, MICHIGAN, UNITED STATES OF AMERICA
1971

Dear Dr. Black,

I wish to dedicate this little book to you as a token of regard. It would be difficult for me to speak too gratefully of the courtesy I have received at your hands. I can cherish no brighter hope for my own ministry than that after a lengthened term of service, such as yours has been, I too may have won some of that loving reverence in which you are held by our noble congregation.

Very truly yours,

G. H. MORRISON.

Wellington Church,
  Glasgow, 1903.

INTRODUCTION

"Dr. George Herbert Morrison has a gift of saying things that we all would have said, had it occurred to us to say them; and he said those inevitable things as we could not, in English prose that had the effect of poetry on the heart." This quotation of James Denney aptly sums up the "secret" — if there was such a thing — of Dr. Morrison's classic sermons delivered from his pulpit in Wellington Church, Glasgow, Scotland, from 1902 to 1928.

Throughout his ministry he was known for his concentrated study, his regular pastoral visitation, and his constant writing for publication. His appeal lay not in any physical stature, for he lacked that; not in any tricks or oratory, for he never preached for effect; but in the quiet winsome way in which he spoke to the heart from a heart suffused with the love and grace of Christ. He never lost sight of the fact that as a minister of Christ his first concern must be how best to bring his hearers closer to the heart of the Lord.

Although some fifty years old now, his sermons are modern in touch and spirit; the tone and temper are admirably effective for use today. Their simplicity of phrase came out of arduous toil as the writer worked in his preparation. The style is the man — quiet and genial — and his preaching was like this. Morrison was always the pastor-preacher, ever seeking to meet life's needs with some word from God.

Whatever he did had the hallmark of preparation and finality. Some sermons came easily like the bird on the wing; others came after much hard work and sweat of mind and heart. The fact that he brooded over his texts with something of an artist's unconsciousness and superb leisure is one of the elements in his power as a preacher. He brooded over the Word of God until it became translucent. His loyalty to Christ and his devotion in the secret place are wedded to his daily practice of study and writing.

His counsel to the young preacher is most revealing as the secret of his own success: "I can think of nothing, except that young preachers will do well to guard against the tendency to rush which is the bane of modern life. The habit of unprofitable bustle and rush, the present-day preoccupation with small affairs and engagements, is withholding many good things from us. For myself it is essential that I have leisure to brood and meditate."

To read and study these selections from the author's many volumes of messages will be to open new vistas of truth and to learn how old and familiar truths can be clothed in fresh and living words which will glow with unsuspected meaning.

Ralph G. Turnbull

GEORGE H. MORRISON, D.D.

It used to be said that just as visitors to London in
bygone days felt that they must of necessity hear
Spurgeon or Parker or Liddon, so visitors to Glasgow
in more recent years had the feeling that they could
not miss hearing Dr. George H. Morrison in Wellington Church. One of the most noted of English Bis-
hops, after fulfilling an afternoon engagement at the
University, hurried off to be in time for the evening
service at Wellington. And the miner from Fifeshire,
or the crofter from the Hebrides, spending a Sunday
in Glasgow, would have considered the day incom-
plete if he did not hear Dr. Morrison.

To Glasgow Dr. Morrison's ministry at Wellington

was something like what Dr. Alexander Whyte's ministry at St. George's was to Edinburgh. Different in many ways, they were alike in the extent to which they captured the community and maintained their unbroken hold year after year.

Dr. Morrison was a great preacher who was also a great pastor. Of this rather unusual combination he was, indeed, the supreme example.

His genius as a preacher was never more clearly shown than by his success in solving the problem of the second service. Shortly after his settlement in Glasgow, the afternoon service was giving place to an evening one, but the results in general were not too satisfactory. When Wellington decided on an evening service Dr. Morrison was determined to give it a distinctive character. In the mornings he adhered to the old Scottish tradition of expository preaching.

In the evenings he allowed himself a wider scope, presenting the Christian essentials in a somewhat different setting, and, as he said, calling to his help every type of illustrative aid that appealed to him. He strove to give these evening addresses a strong human interest, in order, as he put it, "to win the attention, in honourable ways, of some at least of the vast class of people who sit very loosely to the Church. The touch is naturally far lighter than in the morning, but this does not mean lack of preparation. I prepare as carefully for the one as for the other." His one aim in preaching, he once said, was "to help people along the road." Here I may interpolate how Dr. Morrison once told me that, after he had fully prepared his subject, he set himself the task of striving to see how simply he could present it. His simplicity, therefore, was not the easy, facile thing some may have supposed it to be; it was the fruit of definite and earnest effort.

The response at his evening service was immediate and striking. The church became crowded to overflowing, long queues formed in University Avenue before the doors were opened and this was no mere passing phase. The same state of matters continued for over twenty-six years, right to the end of his ministry. And he got the class of people he set out to reach. These crowded evening congregations at Wellington made an interesting study in themselves. All classes and all ages were represented, but young men and women were always largely in evidence. Nor were they there because of the prospect of any novelty or sensation. They could only have been drawn because they felt that their wistful longings and inarticulate yearnings were somehow met and answered by the man in the pulpit with the soft voice, the quiet effortless style, and the subtle elusive charm.

There was no clangorous or challenging presentation of a new Evangel. Dr. Morrison's secret was in taking old familiar truths and clothing them in fresh robes of language which made them sparkle with a lustre of their own and revealed meanings hitherto hidden and unsuspected. He had a perfect flair in the selection of texts often fresh and suggestive. "He gave them drink out of the depths," "In the day that thou stoodest on the other side," "The deep that croucheth beneath," "Thou didst cleave the earth with rivers," are some that may be quoted, almost at random.

Many of his sermons were prose poems; all of them were suffused with a tender charm and rich in spiritual helpfulness. Volume after volume was published, and G. H. Morrison's sermons found a place in manse libraries everywhere, almost like those of F. W. Robertson, of Brighton, while they also very markedly appealed to a wide circle of lay readers. They revealed him to be both a mystic and a man of letters, and were acknowledged to place him in the foremost ranks of British preachers. . . .

There are many people who still remember this or that sermon of Dr. Morrison's; there are as many who love to recall instances of his pastoral devotion. His routine visitation, so extensive and incessant, was but one feature of his pastoral activity. Many tales could be told of his constant solicitous care of the sick and those in sorrow or trouble. And no success or joy that came to any member of any family in his congregation was overlooked or allowed to pass without letters or postcards from him, which are still prized possessions.

The end of this notable ministry came swiftly and unexpectedly when Dr. Morrison was at the age of sixty-two, and while there was no sign of any waning of his powers and no abatement of his popularity. In the first week of October, 1928, he was back from his summer holiday — he held that a good holiday was a *sine qua non* for a minister — and he was getting into the full stream of another winter's activities. On the Wednesday afternoon he had spent three continuous hours in the homes of his people, and in the evening he gave a memorable address to a small company of workers in the hall of Gorbals Church. On Thursday evening he became seriously ill, and on Sunday morning shortly after midnight he passed away, almost before his illness had become generally known.

On the day before he died, when there was a slight rally, he was able to have in his hands one of the early copies of a book to which he had been looking forward — his biography, which I had written at the request of London publishers, and in the preparation of which he had given me every facility with his characteristic kindness.

Although Dr. Morrison did not reach the allotted span, he, if any man, had done what he used to call "a good day's darg." He warned young preachers against unprofitable bustle and rush, and preoccupation with small affairs and trifling engagements. A master of method, he so ordered his time that, while he was never idle, he was never hurried or flurried. There was always about him a calm serenity, and as he moved among men he seemed a living epistle of what he preached.

Reprinted from Alexander Gammie, *Preachers I Have Heard,* Pickering & Inglis, Ltd. (London, n.d.)

CONTENTS

CONTENTS

CONTENTS

THE HOMESICKNESS OF THE SOUL

And when he came to himself, he said, 'How many hired servants of my father's have bread enough and to spare, and I perish with hunger!'—Luke xv. 17.

A VERY fresh and delightful American writer, John Burroughs—a man who often reminds us of our own Richard Jefferies—has given us in one of his books a most illuminative and suggestive paper on Carlyle. Mr. Burroughs visited Carlyle in London—his essay is called ' A Sunday in Cheyne Row '—and with great tenderness, and wisdom, and literary skill he has recorded his impressions of the visit. Now I am not going to speak of Mr. Burroughs to-night, nor am I going to preach about Carlyle ; but there was one phrase in that essay that seemed to me very memorable : it was the phrase ' homesickness of the soul.' 'A kind of homesickness of the soul was on Carlyle,' says Mr. Burroughs, ' and it deepened with age.'

That, then, is the topic on which I wish to speak. My subject is the homesickness of the soul. I want to take the thought that the soul is homesick, and use it to shed a little light on dark places. Perhaps we shall proceed more comfortably together if I divide what I have to say under two heads. (1) Under this light we may view the unrest of sin. (2) Under this light we may view the craving for God.

First, then. Under this light we may view the unrest of sin.

It is notable that it was in this light that Jesus viewed it, in the crowning parable from which we have taken our text. The prodigal was an exile ; he was in a far country. It was the memory of his home that filled his heart. There are conceptions of the awakened sinner that make him the prey of an angry and threatening conscience. And I know that sometimes, when a man comes to himself, he can see nothing and hear nothing in the universe but the terrors and judgments of a sovereign God. But it was not terror that smote the prodigal deep. It was home, home, home, for which his poor soul was crying. He saw the farm, bosomed among the hills, and the weary oxen coming home at eventide, and the happy circle gathered round the fire, and his father crying to heaven for the wanderer. His sorrow's crown of sorrows was remembering happier things. He came to himself, and he was homesick.

Now I think that Jesus would have us learn from that that wickedness is not the home-land of the soul, and that all the unrest and the dissatisfaction of the wicked is just the craving of his heart for home. We were not fashioned to be at home in sin. We bear the image of God, and God is goodness. The native air of this mysterious heart is the love and purity and joy of heaven. So when a man deliberately sins, and all the time hungers for better things, it is not the hunger for an impossible ideal; it is the hunger of his soul for home. Ah! do not forget that you can satisfy that hunger instantly. To-night, out of the furthest country, in a single instant of time, you may come home. We are not like the emigrant in the far west of Canada longing for Highland hills he will not see for years. God waits. Christ says, 'Return this very hour.' Though your sins be as scarlet, they shall be white as snow.

In that very fascinating little volume by Charlotte Yonge, in which she narrates the history of the Moors in Spain, there are few pages more enthralling than those in which she tells the story of Abderraman. Abderraman was the first Moorish Khalif in Spain. He was an Eastern, bred by the Euphrates. There was no great beauty in the scenes where he spent his childhood. And his Spanish home, in the old city of Cordova, seems to have been a fairy-palace of delight. Yet among all the groves and towers and fountains of fair Cordova, Abderraman was miserable—it was banishment. And when he got a palm-tree from his Syrian home, and planted it in his Spanish garden, one of the old baliads of the Arabs tells us that he could never look at it without tears. Do you not think that the children of Cordova would mock at that? It was their home, and they were very happy. They could not understand this Oriental, unhappy and restless among the garden groves. And my point is that you will never understand the soul's unrest, amid the exquisite delights of sense and sin, unless it is hungering for another country, as Abderraman hungered for his Syrian dwelling. It is not facts, it is mysteries, that keep me from materialism. I believe in the cravings of the human heart, and they overturn a score of demonstrations. If I were a creature of a few nerves and fibres only, I should be very happy in my Cordova. But we were made in goodness, and we were made for goodness ; and the native air of the soul is love and truth ; and we shall always be dissatisfied, always be homesick, if we are trying to live in any other land.

This thought, too, helps us to understand why men cover evil with a veil of goodness. It is just the longing of the exile or of the emigrant to give a homelike touch to his surroundings. Why do you find an Inverness in Canada? Because men and women from Inverness went there. And why do you find a Glasgow in Canada ? Because it reminded these Glasgow men of home. Do you know what James Chalmers of New Guinea—the greatest soul on the Pacific, as Stevenson called him—do you remember what he called the first bay he discovered in New Guinea ? He called it Inveraray Bay. I do not think he would ever have dreamed of that name had he not been born and spent his boyhood by Loch Fyne. And when I see men taking the names of goodness and labelling their vices and their sins with them, when I note how ready we all are to use a kindly term for some habit or frailty that is most unkindly, I think that it is the soul telling where it was born, confessing unconsciously that it is a little homesick, and trying to give a homelike touch to the far country, just like James Chalmers with his Inveraray Bay.

And we can understand the loneliness of sin when we remember this homesickness of the soul. The man who is homesick is always lonely. It does not matter how crowded the streets are ; the city may be gay and bright and brilliant, but all the stir of it, and all the laughter of it, and all the throng and tumult of the life of it will not keep a homesick man from being lonely. Nay, sometimes it intensifies his loneliness. It is made more acute by the contrasts of the crowd. It is not in the quiet spaces of great nature, it is among the crowds whom you will meet to-night, that the bitterness of loneliness is found. Now sin is a great power that makes for loneliness. Slowly but surely, if a man lives in sin, he drifts apart into spiritual isolation. And the strange

thing is that the sins we call social sins, the sins
that begin in fellowship and company, are the very
sins that drive a man apart, and leave him at last
utterly alone.   That loneliness is homesickness of
the soul.   It is the heart craving for home again.
God grant that if in this house there be one man
who is drifting away on a great sea of wretched
self-indulgence, from wife and child or mother
and sister and friend—God grant that, drawn by
the love of Christ, he may come home !

Secondly and briefly : Under this light we may
view the craving for God.

We often speak of heaven as our home, and in
many deep senses that is a true expression.   If in
heaven we shall meet again those whom we loved
and lost, and if boys and girls will be playing in
the streets of Zion, I have no doubt that heaven
will be a homelike place.   But in deeper senses
heaven is not our home, or if it is, it is just
because God is there.   In the deepest sense our
home is not heaven, but God.   Do you remember
how Wordsworth put it in his glorious Ode on
the Intimations of Immortality from Childhood ?
I think a lesser poet would have written it thus,
' Trailing clouds of glory do we come from

heaven which is our home.' But Wordsworth, like a true seer, did not write that, but—' Trailing clouds of glory do we come from God, who is our home.'

> ' Our God, our help in ages past,
> Our hope for years to come,
> Our shelter from the stormy blast,
> And—our eternal home.'

God is the true home of the human soul.

Do you see, then, the meaning of that craving for God that is one of the strangest facts in human history? You would have thought that in a world like this, so full of interest, colour, music, and delight, mankind would have lived in contentment without God. But the Book of Psalms is filled with that passionate craving —'As the hart pants after the water-brooks.' And if the Book of Psalms has lived through chance and change, and been cherished when ten thousand volumes are forgotten, it is largely because it gives a voice in noblest poetry to this unappeased hunger of mankind. We do not crave for God because He is glorious. We do not crave for God because He is sovereign. We are just homesick, that is the meaning of it. We crave for God because He is our home.

Now this homesickness of the soul for God is one of our surest proofs of God. It is an argument more powerful than any that philosophy affords to convince me that there is a God. We are all grateful when a prince of science like Lord Kelvin tells us he is forced to believe in a directive power. But in a day or two you will have some one writing to the *Times* denying the validity of that induction. But no one denies that souls still pant for God. And hearts to-day and here still thirst for Him, as truly as the exiled psalmist did. And unless life be a sham, and unless we were born and fashioned to be mocked, there cannot be homesickness without a home. I crave for food, and mother-earth holds out her hands to me and says, 'Yes, child, there is food.' I crave for happiness ; and the shining of the sun, and the song of birds, and the sound of music, and the laughter of children, come to my heart and say to me, 'There it is.' I crave for God. And will the universe reverse its order now ? Will it provide for every other instinct, and call the noblest of them all a mockery ? It is impossible. Without a home, homesickness is inexplicable. My craving for

God assures me that God is. All other arguments may fail me. When my mind is wearied, and my memory tired, I forget them. But this one, knit with my heart, and part and parcel of my truest manhood, survives all moods, is strong when I am weak, and brings me to the door of God my home.

One of the saddest letters in all literature is a letter written by our own poet, David Gray. David Gray was born eight miles from Glasgow; he went to the Free Church Normal in this city. His honest father would have made a preacher of him, but God forestalled that by making him a poet. Well, nothing would satisfy David but he must go to London. He suffered much there and fell into consumption. And this is one of his last letters home :—'TORQUAY, *Jan.* 6, 1861. DEAR PARENTS,—I am coming home — homesick. I cannot stay from home any longer. What's the good of me being so far from home and sick and ill? O God! I wish I were home never to leave it more! Tell everybody that I am coming back—no better: worse, worse. What's about climate, about frost or snow or cold weather, when one's at home? I wish I had

never left it. . . . I have no money, and I want
to get home, home, home. What shall I do, O
God ! Father, I shall steal to you again, because
I did not use you rightly. . . . Will you forgive
me ? Do I ask that ? . . . I have come through
things that would make your hearts ache for me
—things that I shall never tell to anybody but
you, and you shall keep them secret as the grave.
Get my own little room ready quick, quick ;
have it all tidy, and clean, and cosy, against my
homecoming. I wish to die there, and nobody
shall nurse me except my own dear mother, ever,
ever again. O home, home, home ! '

I will arise and go unto my Father. Thank
God we need no money for that journey. Is there
no one here who has been far away, who is going
to come home—to God—this very hour ?

MYSTERY

Now I know in part.—1 Cor. xiii. 12.

IT has ever been a mark of Christianity that it kept men alive to the mysteries around them. The souls that have drunk most deeply of the Christian doctrine are the souls who have most felt the mystery of life. You may gather up the Christian teaching in confessions, and it is vitally necessary that that should be done. But when everything is tabulated and reduced to system, we are still haunted by a sense of the inexplicable—more is meant than meets the ear. I dare say a chemist could explain to me the causes of all the colours in a sunset. And yet in the blending glories of a sunset there is something that no man shall ever analyse. So men have gathered up and set in order the contents of the Christian revelation, but the great secrets have not ceased to baffle them.

And yet, perhaps, there never was a time in

which the sense of mystery was less present than to-day. 'We have not any mysteries to-day,' said a French writer whom I chanced on lately. How far that dying out of the mysterious may be traced to the decline of living faith is a question that might admit of much discussion. But there are other causes which I should like to indicate.

One is the tyranny of facts under which we live. I suppose there was never a time in the world's history when there was such a craving for scientific truth. There is no man more apt to be blind to the great mysteries than the specialist, and this is pre-eminently the age of specialism. Tennyson is most wonderfully accurate in every reference he makes to nature, and in this, as in so many other points, he interprets the spirit of the age he lived in. Now no one will question the value of that spirit, nor the immense gains which it has won for us. I only suggest that an age with that dominant note is not likely to be haunted by the mystery of things.

And then again this is an age of machinery, and there is little mystery in a machine. We are likely to grow dull to many wonders, when we take to calculating by *horse*-power. 'So many

hundred hands in this mill,' says Charles Dickens
in that powerful little story of his, *Hard Times*,
'so many hundred horse steam power. It is
known, to the force of a single pound-weight,
what the engine will do. . . . There is no mystery
in it.' And he means that when an age puts the
emphasis not on man but on machinery, we are
not likely to be troubled greatly by the strange
sense of the inexplicable.

And then this is an age of travel. The world
is explored into its darkest corners. We do not
expect now, as men expected once, to hear of
marvellous things from Africa or India. I love
to turn the pages of Sir John Mandeville, that
most amazing mediæval wanderer. You had only
to cross the sea with Sir John Mandeville, and
you were in the midst of astounding mysteries at
once. But the world is very different to-day.
Its most distant countries have been mapped and
photographed. Knowledge has come, and perhaps a little wisdom with it ; but the older sense
of the world's mystery has gone. 'Ah me !' says
our Scottish poet Alexander Smith, in his most
delightful essay *On Vagabonds*, 'what a world this
was to live in two or three centuries ago, when it
was getting itself discovered. . . . Then were the

Arabian Nights commonplace, enchantments a matter of course, and romance the most ordinary thing in the world. Then man was courting Nature, now he has married her. Every mystery is dissipated.'

I think, then, that it is supremely important in these times that we should endeavour to keep alive the sense of mystery. And I am sure that the Lord Jesus Christ always meant it to have large room in His disciples' hearts.

Think, for example, of what our Lord meant by unbelief. 'Why are ye fearful, O ye of little faith?' That was the one rebuke which He used to launch at His disciples, for there was nothing that grieved Christ more than lack of faith. And it was not lack of faith in any particular doctrines —it was not *that* which called out the rebuke of Christ. It was rather such a view of God's great universe as left no room for any mystery in it. Why are ye fearful, O ye of little faith? Is there nothing else abroad but storm and cloud-rack? Had they only felt the mystery of the Divine, touching and girding even the angry waters, they had been less disquieted, out at sea. That was what Jesus meant by unbelief: not a mind that denies, but a spirit that disowns. A heart that will not recognise, amid things seen, the power, the love, the mystery of God. You see, then, that the disciple of Christ must have a spirit that is alive to mystery.

And then you remember that other declaration : 'Except ye become as little children.' You cannot even see the kingdom of God, unless within you is the heart of childhood, and all things are mysterious to the child. The children's world is full of spiritual presences ; they never think of God as far away. I do not think that any child would be much surprised if it met God out in the green fields. Flowers speak to them in voices we have lost, the night winds cry to them, the clouds are still peopled countries. In the red depths of the winter's fire on the hearth, they see 'mighty castles towering to the moon.' The fear of childhood is not the fear of cowardice ; the fear of childhood is the fear of imagination. We should all fear the darkness as the child does, if we believed it was full of eyes and living things. Now Jesus wants no disciple to be childish : when we become men we put away childish things. But the childlike spirit, that believes in possibilities, that hungers for a world behind the world, that cannot touch a flower or hear an echo but there comes some suggestion of things mystical, *that* spirit is the spirit of the Christian. You see, then, that in the Christian temper Christ Jesus insisted on a large place for mystery. ' Except ye become as little children.'

It is notable, too—I wish to impress this on you—that Jesus deepened the mystery of everything He touched. Things never become less mysterious, always more, when they have passed through the mind and heart of Jesus Christ. We think of Jesus as the great explainer, and we thank God for the rough places Christ has made plain. He has given an answer to a thousand problems. He has come like light into our human darkness. But Jesus never explained anything by lessening the mystery that clung to it. He is a sorry teacher who shows the merely obvious. Jesus enlarged the mystery of things, intensified it, deepened it twentyfold. When He wished to make men understand a matter, He showed that there was more to be understood than they had dreamed.

Take one of His leading words like *life*, for instance. You say, and say rightly, that Christ explains life to you. You understand it better, and you can live it better, in the light that Jesus has cast upon its meaning. But when I think of what life meant in the old pagan world, how shallow it was, how sensuous and short, and when I compare that with the life that is in Christ, with its depth, its joy, its fulness, its infinite issues, I feel at once how the mystery of life is deepened, in passing through the hands of Jesus Christ.

Or take the thought of *death*. Christ has illumined death. There is not a mourner here but has felt, in the dark hour, how unutterably glorious is the gospel teaching. It is when the heart is empty, and the grave is open, that we know the tenderness and power of Christian consolation. Christ has illumined death; but has He banished its mystery? He hath taken away its sting, but deepened its mystery. There are moral bearings in it: it is the wages of sin. There are glorious hopes in it: the body shall be raised. There are dim suggestions in the very word, of eternal separations from love and joy and God. And all this mystery of light, and mystery of darkness, has been poured into the cup of death by Jesus Christ. Death has strange meanings for the humblest now, that it had not for the

wisest before Jesus came. Christ has intensified
its mystery a thousandfold.

Or not to multiply instances, take the thought
of *God*. You and I know God through the
Lord Jesus Christ. All that we know of God
from outward nature, and all that we gather from
the world's long history, is but the outwork and
flanking of that revelation which is ours through
the life and death of Jesus. Now tell me, is God
less mysterious to us in the light of that revelation of Christ Jesus ? 'God without mystery
were not good news.' God was a Sovereign once,
now He is Father, and there are more mysteries
in Fatherhood than in Kingship. God was a God
of power once ; He is a God of love now ; and
all the power of all the thunderbolts of Jove are
not so mysterious as the slightest spark of love.
And God was alone once, or there were many
Gods. Now, baffling comprehension, yet most
real, we have a vision of Three in One and One in
Three. Christ has intensified the mystery of God.

I trust that you see, then, how true it is, that
Jesus deepened the mystery of things. And I
trust that you begin to understand what the spirit
of Christ longs to achieve in you. The Christian

view is always the deepest view.   The Lord who inspired it saw kingdoms in mustard - seeds. There is more in the world, and in man, and in the Bible, than the nicest calculation can discover, but we only see it through the eyes of Christ. They tell us that to see the unusual we ought to travel.   But perhaps a better way to see it is to be Christ's.   For it is then that life, and death, and human hearts, and all things, break into glories of meaning unsuspected.   It is then, too, that a man becomes humble.   Touched by a sense of mystery, he must be reverent.   And it is then that he begins again to wonder ; and when a man ceases to wonder, may God pity him ! Do not be dogmatic.   Do not be bigoted. The world is too mysterious for that.   Expect surprises.   Have an open eye.   Believe that there are more things in heaven and earth than have been dreamed of in your philosophies. And then, when common actions are irradiated, and common lives flash into moral glories, when the mysteries of life, and love, and death, and God, so baffle us that we can only say with Paul ' we know in part '—we shall be nearer the spirit of Jesus than we dreamed.

'THE WONDER AND BLOOM OF THE WORLD'

Consider the lilies of the field.—Matt. vi. 28.

IN these glorious June days, when the world is so full of light and joy, it is an unspeakable satisfaction to remember that our Lord was keenly alive to the message of nature. It is part of the undying charm of the gospel-story that while it sounds all the deeps of the human spirit, it never forgets that we are living in a world where the grass is green and where the birds are singing. There are poets whose gift is that of interpreting nature. There are others whose genius works at its noblest in interpreting the strange story of mankind. But the sublimest masters are dowered with both these gifts—they interpret nature and they interpret man. Now Jesus Christ was far more than a poet; He was inspired as no poet ever was. Yet the twofold gift of interpreting nature and man, the gift that is the glory of our masterpieces, shines out most cloudlessly upon the gospel-page. It is there we read of the Samaritan woman. It is there we read of the denial of Peter. But the mustard-seed and the birds and the lilies are there too.

Now no doubt this love of nature which was so strong in Jesus sprang partly from the circumstances of His birth. He was a Hebrew with a Hebrew lineage, after the flesh, and nature was eloquent with voices to the Hebrew. You can often tell what a people gives its heart to by the richness and copiousness of its vocabulary. Where a nation's interests have been long and deeply engaged, there it soon wins for itself a wealth of terms. Well, in the Hebrew language there are some ten words for rain, and to the understanding heart that is significant. Into that heritage, then, Jesus of Nazareth entered. He was the child of a race that had lived with open eyes. And if the glory of the world lights up the gospel-story—if there are sermons in stones, and books in running brooks, there, we owe it in some measure to God's ordering, when He cradled Emmanuel in a Hebrew home.

But between the Hebrew outlook on nature

in the Old Testament, and the outlook of Jesus as we find it in the gospels, there is one marked difference that we cannot note too closely. There is one contrast which no one can fail to remark, who reads the prophets and the psalms and then turns to the gospels. In the psalms the world is magnificent and terrible. It is a mighty pageant of grand and mysterious forces. We see the sun there rejoicing like a strong man to run his race ; we hear the rush of the storm as it shatters the cedars of Lebanon. The sea is angry, its waves mount up to heaven. There is the roll of thunder ; there is the flash of lightning. You feel that clouds and darkness are never far away. It is a vast and glorious world—hardly a kindly one. Now turn to the gospels, and do you note the change ? Consider the lilies of the field, the fowls of the air. Behold the sower goes forth to sow in the spring morning. The kingdom of heaven is like a mustard-seed. It is not that vast and magnificent things are disregarded, and the beauty of the small things recognised. That is not what gives us the sense of contrast between the nature of the psalmist and of Jesus. It is rather that the world is a much kindlier place ; there is less menace in its terrific powers. It is still as full of mystery as ever ; but it is the mystery of love now, not of fear.

Now can we explain that deep and striking change ? It is quite clear that nature will not explain it. Had Jesus lived under a sunnier sky or amid fairer pastures than the old Hebrew psalmists, we might think that the change was due to change of scene. But the same stars looked down on Jesus of Nazareth as touched into music the craving heart of David ; and the same wild storms leapt out of the blue heaven as have given the fire and rush to Hebrew melody. And the hills and the streams and the gleaming of the sea far off, these were the same. It is clear, then, that there is no explanation there.

Nor is there any—I speak with loving reverence of One to whom I owe so much—nor is there any explanation in the change of persons. I mean that had the lot of Jesus been a kindly lot, I could have fathomed His kindly view of nature. Has not Tennyson sung very wisely and very well—

'Gently comes the world to those
That are cast in gentle mould'?

and had the life of Jesus been a life of ease and

tenderness, I think I could explain his view of nature. But did He not come unto His own and they received Him not? Was He not despised and rejected of men? Were there no drops of sweat like blood in lone Gethsemane? Was there no cup to drink, no cross to bear and die on? I do not think that bitter sorrows like these make a man ready to consider the lilies. In my own tragedies the world grows tragical. I understand the storm when I am storm-tossed. But to Jesus, misunderstood, cross-burdened, Man of Sorrows, nature was genial, kindly, homelike, to the end.

Here is the explanation of that contrast. It is not change of scene, nor change of circumstance. It is the changed thought of God that is the secret. To prophet and psalmist, no less than to Jesus, the world was alive and quivering with God. But to prophet and psalmist God was Jehovah; to Jesus of Nazareth God was Father. Twelve times over in this sixth chapter of Matthew Christ speaks of the Creator as 'your Father.' I have read of the child of a distinguished English judge who was rebuked for prattling beside the judge's knee. And the bairn answered : 'Why should I not? He may be your judge, but he's my father.' So when the thought of the Creator, infinite in majesty, was deepened and softened and glorified in Fatherhood, the mystery of fear was swept out of the world, and the gentle mystery of love came in. It was a Father who had reared the mountains. There was a Father's hand upon the storm. At the back of the thunder, no less than in the lilies, there was a Father's heart, a Father's love. It was that glorious truth filling the heart of Jesus that made all nature what it was for Him. Perfect love had cast out fear.

In the city of Florence there is an old building now used as a museum. Six hundred years ago it was a palace, and on the altar wall of its chapel, sometime about 1300, Giotto painted a portrait of the poet Dante. This portrait, the only one painted during the poet's lifetime, is of inestimable value. But the building fell upon evil days; it was turned into a jail for common criminals; its walls were coated with whitewash. And for centuries under this covering the face of Dante was hidden, until its existence was wellnigh forgotten. But in 1840 three gentlemen, one of them an Englishman, set to work and discovered the lost likeness. And now the old prison-wall is full of glory because the lineaments of the great poet shine out there. Ah, yes, if a common wall is quite transfigured when the likeness of Dante is discovered on it, no wonder that a common flower is glorified when it reveals—as it did to Christ—the Father. It is a great thing to be alive to beauty ; but men were alive to beauty before Jesus lived. It is a great thing to feel the mystery of nature ; but men had felt all that in paganism. What Jesus did was to take the truth of Fatherhood, and touch every bird and every lily with it, till beauty deepened into brotherhood, and we and the world were mystically kin. 'When I consider the heavens,' said the psalmist, 'then say I, what is man that Thou art mindful of him?' But Jesus, just to reassure us of God's mindfulness, says, 'Consider the lilies of the field.'

Such, then, was the secret of nature for our Lord. And now I have a word to say upon one other point. I want you to observe how constantly and simply our Lord used nature in the interests of morals. Our outlook on nature is very largely emotional. We make it a mirror to reflect our moods. If we are happy, then all the

world is happy.   But if we are sad, then even the
banks and braes o' bonny Doon 'mind me o'
departed joys, Departed—never to return.'   Now
all that is very natural, I doubt not; and it is a
witness to the grandeur of our human story that
we make every stream and every sunset echo it.
But in the life of Jesus there is little of that; it
is the moral helpfulness of nature that He seizes.
Burns wondered how the flowers could bloom
when he was so weary.   That is the emotional
outlook on the world.   Tennyson said: 'Flower
in the crannied wall, could I but understand thee,
I should know what God and man is.'   That is
the intellectual outlook on the world.   But Jesus
said : 'Why take ye thought for raiment?   Consider the lilies of the field,' and that is neither
emotional nor intellectual ; it is moral.   I do not
mean that Jesus was blind to the other aspects ;
but I do mean that He centred His thought on
that.   For the soul and the life and the individual
character—these things were so transcendently
important to Christ Jesus, that everything else
must be impressed into their service.   In these
glorious June days we are apt to grow a little dull
to what is highest.   Just to be alive is such a

sweet thing now, that the hope and the resolve of sterner moods take to themselves wings and fly away. Do not forget the earnestness of Christ. Do not forget that out in the summer fields this was His aim—to fashion noble, trustful, reverent disciples. We must have room for the lilies of the field no less than for Gethsemane ; we must remember the birds not less than the bread and wine, if the whole ministry of Christ is to be operative in winning us to some likeness of Himself.

It is notable, too, that as Jesus' life advanced, and as the shadows upon His path grew darker, we find no trace that Jesus outgrew nature, or passed beyond the power of its teaching. I think we have most of us had hours when nature seemed to desert us. She became dumb and had no healing for us. It may have been the hour of a great sorrow, or a great crisis in our life's career. And I think that most of us have had moods and feelings which we thought that nature was powerless to interpret. She could not enter into our weary problems. So as our life goes on we drift away from nature, and nature silently drifts away from us. But what I want you to note is that though that happens with us, there is no trace that it ever happened with Jesus. Here on the hillside He is speaking of providence, and He says, 'Consider the lilies of the field.' Then follows the preaching of the kingdom throughout Galilee, and 'the kingdom of heaven is like a mustard-seed.' Then the shadow of Calvary falls, and the awful death that is coming—can nature interpret and illuminate that darkness? 'Except a corn of wheat fall into the ground and die, it abideth alone.' And where did Christ agonise? Was it in the upper room? He went into a place where was a garden. And in the exultant joy of resurrection morning, did He hasten away into the city? He waited till Mary supposed He was the gardener. Right on, then, through the wealth of all His teaching, right on through His suffering and death and rising, the voices of the natural world appealed to Jesus. Nature may seem to fail us before the end, but it never deserted Jesus Christ.

And the reason is not very far to seek. 'I came to do Thy will, O God.' It was the childlike heart, absolutely true, never swerving by a hair's-breadth from the line of duty, it was His perfect obedience to a Father's will that kept Jesus in perfect touch with His Father's world.   Do you remember how Wordsworth, speaking of the man who does his duty, says:

> ' Flowers laugh before thee in their beds
> And fragrance in thy footing treads ' ?

He means that nature ceases to be musical when we are anywhere else than on the path of duty. Here, then, is the secret of a happy summer, in which all the world and you shall be in comradeship.   It is to be patient, brave, unselfish, kind, and loyal.   It is to accept the cross.   It is to be true.   To see the beautiful, you must be dutiful. It is a most strange world.   ' Blessed are the pure in heart, for they shall see God '—even in the lilies of the field.

MISTAKEN MAGNITUDES

Ye blind guides, which strain at a gnat, and swallow a camel.—
Matt. xxiii. 24.

It was one great complaint of our Lord against
the Pharisees, that they had lost the relative
magnitude of things. They were very much in
earnest about that Jewish law ; but for all that
they had sadly misinterpreted the law. They
laid great stress upon the infinitely little, until
the weightier matters of it passed out of sight.
They magnified trifles—husbanded their rush-
lights till they forgot that the stars were in the
sky. It is that spirit which Jesus is rebuking in
the familiar proverb of our text. Ye blind guides,
(this is what He means) cannot you see that some
things are great and some are little? If there are
larger and lesser lights in the great heavens, will
there not be kindred differences in God's other
firmaments? It is the evil of not seeing things
in true proportion that is present to the mind of
Jesus Christ.

Now it is on that subject that I wish to speak
to-night ; for one of the great arts of worthy
living is to see things in their relative importance.
I have known so many who failed in what was
worthiest, not because they were weaker than
their neighbours—for the strongest of us is piti-
fully weak—they failed not because they were
weaker than the others, but because they never
seemed able to grasp the difference between things
that were really great and really little.   Mr.
Froude, in his *Spanish Story of the Armada*,
makes a significant remark about the Spanish
king.   He is showing the incompetence of
Philip ii., and he says : 'the smallest thing and
the largest seemed to occupy him equally.'   That
was one mark of Philip the Second's incompetence.
That gave the worst of all possible starts to the
Armada.   And for the equipping of nobler vessels
than these galleons, and the fighting of sterner
battles than they fought, that spirit spells incom-
petency still.   It is a great thing to know a trifle
when you meet it.   It is a great thing to know that
gossamer is gossamer.   It is equally great, when
the decisive moment comes, to seize it and use it
with every power of manhood.   It is such swift

distinguishing between the great and little, such vision of the relative magnitude of things, that is one secret of a quiet and conquering life.

Now I think that this gift of seeing things in their true magnitudes is very difficult to exercise to-day. We live in such a hurried fashion now, that we have little leisure to take these moral measurements. When I am travelling sixty miles an hour in the express, I have very hazy thoughts about the country. Villages, towns, meadows, woods, go flashing by, but the speed is too fierce for accurate observing. So with our lives to-day; they hurry forward so. The morning paper has hardly been unfolded, when the children are crying the evening paper in the streets. The wide world's news comes crowding in on us ; we are spectators of an endless panorama. And all this change, and movement, and variety, while it makes men more eager, more intense and responsive, is not conducive to a well-balanced judgment. We are a great deal sharper now than men were once. I do not think we are a great deal deeper. It is the still waters that run deep, and stillness is hardly a characteristic of the city. I have often been humbled, when I lived among them, at the wise judgment of some Highland shepherd. The man was not clever ; he read little but his Bible ; his brilliant son was home with his prizes from college, and I dare say, in the eyes of his brilliant son, the father was fifty years behind the times. But you get the shepherd on to moral questions, on to the relative magnitude of things, and spite of all the Greek and Latin of the prize-winner—and the father is infinitely proud of these bright eyes—spite of the Greek and Latin of the son, you recognise the father as the greater man. Something has come to him amid the silent hills ; the spirit of the lonely moor has touched him ; he has wrestled with a few great truths, a few great sorrows, alone, amid the rolling miles of heather. And it is that discipline of thoughtful quietude, controlling and purifying the moral judgment, that puts the keenest intellect to shame.

This failure to see things in their true proportions is often seen in relation to our grievances. When a man has a grievance—and many men have them—he is almost certain to have distorted vision. You can block out the sun by the smallest coin if you hold the coin near enough to the eye. And we have a way of dwelling on our grievances, till we lose sight of the blue heaven above us. How ready we are to brood on petty insults ! How we take them home with us and nurse and fondle them ! How we are stung by trifling neglects ! A little discourtesy, and our soul begins to fester ! And though hearts are just as warm to us to-day as they were yesterday, when we responded to them ; and though the great tides of the deep love of God rise to their flood, still, on every shore, it is strange how a man will be blind to all the glory, when a little bitterness is rankling within. We are all adepts at counting up our grievances. Open a new column and count your mercies now. It is supremely important to see things in their magnitudes, and perhaps you have never learned that lesson yet. The man who suspects is always judging wrongly. A jealous woman sees everything out of focus. If there be any virtue, if there be any praise, think on these things, says the apostle.

Of course I am aware that the failure to see things in their true proportions has sometimes got physical and not moral roots. There come days when the grasshopper proves itself a burden, and the simple reason is that we are weary. Let a man be vigorous, and strong, and well, and he can take the measurement of his worries very easily. But when he is fagged with the winter toil of a great city we know what alarming proportions trifles take. It is well that a man should remember in such moments that this is the body of our humiliation. Christ understood that matter thoroughly—'Come ye apart,' He said, 'and rest awhile.' The disciples were overstrung and overwrought, and the tact and tenderness of Jesus dealt with that. What the men wanted was a little rest. Never accept the verdict of your weariness. Never judge anything when you are tired. We are so apt to be jaundiced and think bitter things, when all that we want is a little rest and sunshine. All that will come, the birds will sing again ; the dew of May morning will sparkle on the grass. We shall see things in their true proportions then. Meantime trust thou in God, and play the man.

In this connection, too, I find a gleam of glory in the beneficent effects of sleep. Of all the secondary ministries of God for helping us to see things as they are, there is none quite so wonderful as sleep. We go to rest troubled, perplexed, despondent. We cannot see how we shall get through at all. But when we waken, how different things are! Sleep has knit up the ravelled sleeve of care. Now, Jesus loved to speak of death as sleep. He seems to have kept that word death in reserve, as the name for something darker and more terrible. Tennyson talks of ' the death that cannot die,' and I think that is what Jesus meant by death. Our ' death,' for Christ, was sleep, and sleep is the passage to a glad awaking. Shall not *that* sleep do for us what to-night's will do, and help us to see things truly in the morning? Then we shall know even as we are known. There will be no mistaken magnitudes in heaven. There will be no errors in proportion there. We shall no longer be blind to the relative importance of things that confused us when we fell asleep. The love at home that we despised down here, and the selfishness that made those whom we loved unhappy, and the work we tried to do with so much failure, and the exquisite joys, and the bitterness of tears—all these we shall see at last in their true magnitudes when we awaken in the eternal morning.

Meantime we are on this side of the grave.

There are heavy mists lying along the valley. I want to ask, then, what are the gospel powers that help a man to see things as they are?

First, then, remember that the gospel which we preach puts love at the very centre of our life. It makes all the difference what you put first and foremost, and the gospel of Jesus Christ puts love there. That was the tragedy of these poor Pharisees. It is always a tragedy when love dies out. When anything else than love is at the centre, the gnats and the camels are certain to get mixed. For love alone sees purely, clearly, deeply. Love always seeks the best interpretation. Love never makes the most of petty faults. The windows of love are of the finest glass. And it is that spirit of loving interpretation that helps a Christian to see things as they are. If without love I never can know God, then without love I never can know anything. For every blackthorn that breaks into snow-white blossom, and every bird that is winging its way from Africa, and every human heart, however vile, has something of the Creator in its being. Take away God, and things are chaos to me. And without love, I never can know God. You understand,

then, the wisdom of Jesus Christ in putting love
at the centre of our life. It focuses everything.
It links the little and the great with the Creator,
and brings things to their relative importance.

And then the gospel takes our threescore years
and ten and lays them against the background of
eternity. And a life is like a painting in this
respect, a great deal depends upon the background. Are there any artists here to-night?
You have been charged with making your
colouring too strong. Men say it is a beautiful
and powerful picture, but the hill, and the sunset, and the breaking waves, were never so intense
and vivid as that. The likelihood is that they are
far more vivid ; but the hills and the sunsets are
not *framed*, in nature. Your canvas has got to
end abruptly ; but nothing in nature ever ends
like that. Things stretch away into infinite dis-
tances there. There is not a tree and there is
not a wave but is part of the one grand colour-
scheme of God. And it is because you have to
isolate a little part, and take it out of its setting in
the expanse, that men will tell you sometimes it is
exaggerated. Do you not think the same charges
will be made when we isolate our threescore years

and ten ? The colours will always be too bright,
too dark, unless we remember the eternal setting.
And it is because Christ has brought immortality
to light that the Christian sees things in their true
proportions. I bid you remember that eternal
prospect. The efforts and strivings of our threescore years are not adjusted to the scale of seventy,
they are adjusted to the scale of immortality.
This life is not the opera, it is the overture.
It is not the book, it is the first chapter of the
book. A man must be wakeful to his eternal
destiny if he would know the magnitude of
things.

And then the gospel brings us into fellowship
with Christ, and that is our last great lesson in
proportion. The heart that takes its measurements from Jesus is likely to be pretty near
the truth. A great deal depends on the kind
of company you keep, as to what things are
to be important to you, and what not. It is
one of the hardest tasks of every earnest man
quietly to scorn the measurements of the world,
and in that task we are mightily helped by Christ.
His comradeship reinforces the true standards.
There is a scale of worth in the teaching of Christ

Jesus to which the spirit instantly responds. Cherish that comradeship. Live in that glorious presence. Take your measure of the worth of things from the Redeemer. And when the journey is over, and the hill is climbed, and you look back out of the cloudless dawn, I think you will find that in the fellowship of Christ you have been saved from many a mistaken magnitude.

LAUGHTER AND SORROW

Even in laughter the heart is sorrowful.—Prov. xiv. 13.

FEW men have had larger experience of life than
Solomon, and few have directed a more penetrating gaze on the strange drama that was unfolding
round them. The court of kings is a proverbial
theatre of human nature, and Solomon was
familiar with court life all his days. He had
known saints of God like his own father David.
He had been in touch with men and women of
all nations. Our text, then, is not the utterance
of a recluse, but of one who had large experience
of humanity.

And it is notable that, for the writers of His
Bible, it was such men whom God generally chose.
It was not hermits, nor men who dwelt apart
from the great stir, who were honoured by Heaven
to be Heaven's penmen. It was men who had
known the strain and stress of living, who had
borne the burdens of that complex task, who

had entered largely into the joy and sorrow that blend in the light and shadow of the crowd. Moses was no stranger to the rich life of Egypt. David had passed from shepherding to kingship. The prophets of Israel were inspired statesmen, intensely alive to the needs and to the trend of the national life in which they found themselves. And Paul was at home in any company.

Now do you see the reason of this choice of instruments ? I do not think that it is far to seek. It is that we might catch the accent of a brother's voice, and feel the impress of a brother's hand, in the Word divine which comes to lead us heavenward. The greatest books do not speak to us as strangers. They are not voices from regions where we have never journeyed. They interpret and illuminate these inarticulate longings in us, which crave for utterance yet cannot find it. And the Bible is the greatest of the great in that sense, that it pulsates and throbs with sweet and mysterious brotherhood. It was vitally necessary, if this book were to grip, that it should not reach the heart as something alien. And one of God's methods for making that impossible was to use Solomon and the prophets and Paul as messengers.

So to our text then.   And there are three
truths that flash on me out of it.   The first is
the difference between outward and inward life.
Even in laughter—Hark! how it rings and
echoes!   Is it not the sign and index of a cloudless heart?   But even in laughter, says Solomon,
the heart is sorrowful.   He is thinking of the
duality of life.

Now that is one of the discoveries we make
with growing intimacy.   It is part of the joy, and
part of the pain, of friendship, that it comes to
find under the outward habit a world of things
it never suspected once.   No men or women
worthy of the name would wear their heart upon
their sleeve 'for daws to peck at.'   There is a
reserve which is inseparable from true dignity,
in the common intercourse of daily life.   But as
intimacy ripens the barriers are broken, glimpses
are had of things we never dreamed of ; there
are hills that reach heavenward, and valleys strewn
with boulders, there are ripening harvests, and
gardens with a grave in them, all in the mystical
country of the heart ; and we were walking in
darkness and we never saw them, till the sunrise
of friendship quickened in the east.   You never

would have thought, when you first met him, that
that rough and rude and somewhat boisterous
man had a heart as tender as a little child's.
And you may meet a woman casually twenty
times, and she is always bright and always
interested ; it is only long afterwards that you
discover that there was a shrouded cross and a
hidden sorrow there. That, then, is one of the
gains and pains of friendship : it reveals to us the
duality of life.

Now in all our Lord's dealing with men and
women we feel that this difference between the
outward and the inward was before Him. You
will not grasp the influence of Jesus, in all its
wonderful impact on mankind, unless you bear in
mind this strange duality. I do not refer to the
methods of our Saviour in dealing with those who
were consciously insincere. Christ unmasked
hypocrites instantly and terribly : the Light was
far too strong for that disguise. What I mean
is that under all outward seeming our Lord
discerned the struggle of the heart ; He was
never misled by laughter or by speech ; He
never ignored all that we cannot utter. And
if the woman of Samaria felt that she had found

a friend ; if Zaccheus was not despised, nor
Matthew scorned ; if the lawless and intractable
zealot was redeemed ; if Peter was ransomed and
rescued from himself—there was the insight of
love in it, the genius of the heart ; there was
the knowledge that life is deeper, richer, sadder,
than is ever to be gathered from a surface-
view.

That, then, is the first truth in our text.   The
second is this : Sorrow and joy are strangely knit
together.   Even in laughter the heart is sorrowful.

If you have ever lived in a little town or
village you know how life is intermingled there.
The classes are not separated as in the cities ;
they blend insensibly into one another.   Children
of all stations go to school together ; the better-
off have companions in very humble homes ;
the banker and the blacksmith will be excellent
friends.

Now all that intermingling of a more primitive
life resembles the intermingling of our being.
We are each of us knit together into unity by
bonds too subtle for any to detect.   How often
a man's faults are virtues in excess !   How all

that is darkest interweaves with what is brightest! It is that intermingling of the light and shadow that makes the moral government of life so intricate. And could anything be more opposed than joy to sorrow? There seems to be a broad world between the two. The one is sunshine, the other is cloud. The one is music, the other is a cry. The one is the summer-time bathed in warmth and light, the other is the wailing of the wind in the late autumn. Surely there can be no kinship of these two? Ah, yes! even in laughter the heart is sorrowful. There is a mystical union between our smiles and tears. Solomon saw, what you and I have seen, that sorrow and joy are strangely knit together.

We see this in the lives of our greatest men, for instance. It is one of the lessons we learn from great biographies. The greatest are very seldom solemn, and certainly they are almost never joyless. Mohammed had drunk deep of the sorrows of mankind, yet 'Mohammed,' says a Scottish professor in a very charming essay, 'Mohammed had that indispensable requisite of a great man, he could laugh.' Luther was plunged into a sea of trouble, yet the laughter of Luther was notoriously boisterous. The latest biographer of Lord Tennyson—Sir Alfred Lyall —says that the laughter of Tennyson was triumphant ; yet it was Tennyson who wrote the *In Memoriam*. True joy is not the mere escape from sorrow. It may be that the capacity for gladness is but the other side of the capacity for pain. In the lives of the greatest, then, we learn this lesson, that sorrow and joy are strangely knit together.

We find this also in our own greatest moments, when the fire of life flashes up in some fierce intensity. When the heart throbs, and feeling is enkindled, and every nerve is quivering with emotion, we scarcely know if we are sorry or glad. It is a master-touch of our master dramatist that in the very heart of his tragedies you will have some fool or jester. It means far more than a mere relief from the agony ; it means that the light and the shadow are akin. Has no one, after some great hour, said this to you : 'I did not know whether to laugh or cry ' ? It ought to have been an hour of exquisite gladness, and in the midst of the gladness came the tears. I see from the newspapers that this is a great time for marriages; and if there is any day in life that should be cloudless, would you not expect it to be the day of bridal? Yet even in the marriage-service comes the shadow, 'Until God shall separate the twain by death.' That, then, is one mark of our greatest hours. They intermingle and interfuse these opposites. There have come moments to every one of us, when sorrow and joy were strangely knit together.

And do you not think that is true of Jesus Christ? It is one of the mysteries of that perfect life. He was a Man of sorrows and acquainted with grief; His soul was exceeding sorrowful, even unto death. Yet through it all, and in the midst of it, our adorable Lord is talking of His joy. Do you remember the Mount of Transfiguration? Was it not an hour of spiritual glory? Whatever else it was, and it was much else, it was the herald and harbinger of resurrection gladness. Yet even in that hour there was the agony: they spake of the decease He should accomplish at Jerusalem. 'My joy' —and yet He was the Man of sorrows. 'My peace'—and yet 'Why hast Thou forsaken Me?'

Sorrow and joy are strangely knit together in the human experience of Jesus Christ.

That, then, is the second truth. And now, very briefly, the third and the deepest is this. Sorrow lies nearer to the heart of life than joy. Even in laughter the heart is sorrowful : at the back of all there is the heart's unrest.

Now I think that even language bears this out; and language becomes very illuminative when we study it. We never talk about a heavy joy : we only talk about a heavy grief. Happiness bubbles up or ripples over ; there is some suggestion of the surface in it. But sorrow is heavy, and what that implies is this, that when God casts it into the sea of life it sinks by its own weight into the deeps. Joy is most real, thank God, intensely real. It is only the pessimist who would call joy a mockery. But underneath all laughter is a pain, a craving that gnaws, a sorrow we cannot baffle ; even in our language there is the sad suggestion that sorrow lies nearer to the heart of life than joy.

I sometimes think that our Lord had this in mind when He said in His sermon, ' Blessed are they that mourn.' They were to be comforted in far other and nobler ways than any one on that hillside understood. The mourner is blessed, not merely because hands may be held out to him, and not because the roughest may grow kind. But he is blessed because sorrow sounds the deeps, and if rightly taken makes the surface-life impossible. For sorrow lies nearer to the heart of life than joy, and to get near life's heart is always blessed.

But whether that be so or not, this one thing I see clearly. Unless this proverb of Solomon prove itself true, the cross is not life's true inter-pretation. In the centre of history stands the cross of Calvary, and the cross is the epitome of woe. And if life's deepest secret be gladness and not sorrow, if laughter run deeper into the heart than tears, then the cross, that professes to touch the deepest depths, can be nothing but a tragical mistake. I do not think that we have found it so. I do not think that the cross has ever failed us. The deepest music that our heart ever uttered has blended and chimed with the sad strain of Calvary. It is a great thing to have a man like Solomon telling us that even in laughter the heart is sorrowful. But it is greater still to have a risen Saviour, who sealed that in the sorrow of the Cross.

THE PAGAN DUTY OF DISDAIN

Take heed that ye despise not one of these little ones.—
Matt. xviii. 10.

IT has often been noticed that the spirit of
contempt is very strongly developed among
savage races. A savage is nurtured to hate or
to despise. Between his own tribe and every
other tribe there is a deep and quite impassable
gulf, and it has never entered into the savage
heart that love or kindness should seek to bridge
that chasm. If other tribes are powerful they
must be hated. If they are weak they must be
treated with contempt. It is one article, then,
in the sad creed of every savage, that there is
virtue in despising others.

And when we pass from the wild life of
savagery to the civilisations of the ancient
world, the remarkable thing is that we are immediately confronted with the same spirit of
contemptuous disdain. We might have hoped

that the culture of the Greek, and his swift appreciation of all things of beauty, would have given him a large sympathy with mankind. We might have expected that the world-conquering Roman, strong in his masculine sense of law and order, would have been too large-hearted to belittle. And above all, we might have trusted that the Jew, to whom had been granted the vision of the eternal, would have learned in the great glory of that vision to call nothing common or unclean. But history tells us a very different story. The old world is flooded with the spirit of contempt. And we do not need to go beyond the Bible story to learn how the Greek looked down on the barbarian, or how the Jew disdained the Gentile world. Everywhere, then, where the spirit of Christ is not, we are confronted with the spirit that contemns. A Christless world, if it believes in anything, believes in the holy duty of disdaining. And it is like the courage of the Lord Jesus Christ that He dared to lift up His voice against the past, to charge it with error in its cherished virtues, to tell it it had gone utterly astray. For all this our blessed Lord was doing, when He taught the lesson of not despising others.

Of course we must distinguish this despising from what I might call the passion of noble scorn. A man is a poor creature and a poorer Christian, if he has lost his capacity for scorn. There are deeds that a right-thinking man will scorn to do. There are books that an earnest heart will scorn to read. And there are men and women whom a heaven-touched soul would scorn to number in its list of friends. A man is out of line with Jesus Christ who cannot kindle into scorn of anything. For if ever in the world there was the passion of scorn, it was in the heart of Jesus in the Temple, when He raised His whip and drove the traders out. Such scorn as that is a very holy thing. It is the kindling of a man's best into a flame. It is all that is purest and most divine within us raised to white-heat by intolerable evil. And a man must be very luke-warm for the right, and have sadly confused weakness with charity, who is never stirred so in a world like this. But to despise is something very different. There is nothing of moral passion in despising. It does not spring from any love of goodness. It is not rooted in any hate of wrong. True scorn is an utterly self-forgetful

thing.   But the man who despises is always full of
self.

And I think it is not difficult to see the evil
that is wrought by the spirit of contempt.   It was
as the champion of the weak and the oppressed,
and that they might have an atmosphere to grow
in, that our Lord spoke so sternly of despising.
It is easy to be good when we are loved.   It is
not very hard to play the man when we are hated.
But to be courteous, charitable, gentle, loving,
kind, when all the time we know we are despised,
is a task that would try the powers of an angel.
There is nothing so likely to make a brother
despicable, as just to let him see that you despise
him.   There is nothing so certain to touch the
flowers with frost-bite, and chill the air, and make
the spirit bitter.   And I think that Jesus Christ
hated contempt, and banished it imperiously from
the kingdom, that chilled and suppressed hearts
might have a chance.   There is only one thing
worse than being despised by others.   And that
is to be despised by one's own self.

And let me say in passing that we must bear
that in mind if we would really know the beauty
of Christ's character.   The wonder of it is

deepened a thousandfold for me, when I remember that He was despised. If it is hard for
you to hold fast to lovely and lowly things, if
it is difficult to be good and to be tender, when
in the eyes that look on you you see contempt,
you may be sure it was not less hard for Jesus.
Nay, on the contrary, it was far harder; for
Jesus was far more sensitive than you. We
have all been dulled and coarsened by our sin;
Jesus alone knew nothing of that coarsening.
In looks that we could never have interpreted,
in words whose sting we never should have felt,
Christ felt in its bitterness that He was despised:
yet what can match the beauty of His character?
Had it been only antagonism that confronted
Him, I think I could understand Christ Jesus
better. For a man is often roused by fierce
antagonism till all his slumbering powers take the
field. But that Jesus of Nazareth should have
wakened every morning and said to His heart,
I shall be despised to-day; that He should
have gone every evening to His rest saying
to His heart, To-day I was despised; and that
in spite of that He should have moved on to
the cross, brave, tender, loving—that is the great

mystery for me. May it not have been because
our Lord knew to its uttermost the temptations
of the soul that is despised, that He spoke so
strongly on not despising others?

Now what are the sources of this contemptuous
spirit? Why is it we are so ready to despise?
Well, I take it that contempt has two main roots,
and the first of them is want of understanding.
There is a great text in Job of which I often think;
it occurs where Elihu is justifying God to men.
And he says, 'God is mighty and despiseth not
any; He is great in strength of understanding.'
Now Elihu was not a very brilliant person; one
can hardly imagine even patient Job listening
patiently to Elihu's preaching. But I could
forgive Elihu a whole volume of commonplace
for this one thought that flashed on his poor
brain. For Elihu means that just because God
is great, and knows each separate heart with
perfect knowledge, and reads, without an error
in one syllable, the intricate story of the worst
and weakest, because of *that*, God is a God of
pity : 'He is mighty and despiseth not any.'
That means that if we knew our brother as God
knows him, we should never dare to despise him

any more. In the last analysis man may be a
sinner, but in the last analysis—thank God—
man is not despicable. If only we knew what
the weakest and worst had borne, if only we
understood how they were tempted, if we could
read the story of their secret battle, could fathom
their wretchedness, could hear their cry ; if
only we realised that under that dull exterior
there are heaven, hell, loneliness, cravings, love,
I think we should cease despising in that
hour. God understands all that, and therefore
despises no one. We despise because we do not
know.

And then the other root is want of love.
Where love is, there can be no contempt.
A man may have twenty despicable traits, but
to the one who loves him he is still a hero.
And that is why, in the love of Christian homes,
men who are not thought much of in the city
are sometimes wonderfully good and gentle.
They are not hypocrites. It is the absence of
even the suspicion of contempt at home that
brings out all that is best and brightest in them.
I have seen a deformed or crippled little boy or
girl sadly despised in the playground and the

street. They have had to stand many a bitter
jest—for children can be terribly cruel. But
though all the playground despise the shrunken
limbs, and make very merry at the arrested brain,
there is one at home who would sooner lie down
in her grave, than think of despising that little
shattered frame. Where a mother's love is, there
is no contempt. It is want of love, then, and
want of understanding, that lie at the roots of
most of our despising. And the question I wish
to ask in closing is this : How does the gospel of
Jesus combat that ? Christ never says do this, and
leaves us there. When He commands, He gives
the power to fulfil. And I wish to ask what are
these powers, that have been called into action by
the Christian gospel, to banish the contemptuous
spirit from the kingdom ?

First, then, there is the height of the ideal that
dawns on a man when he becomes a Christian.
In his new standards of the measurements of
things, there is less difference between him and
others than he thought. A little green hillock
of some thirty feet high might well despise the
molehill in the field. But place them both under
the shadow of Ben Nevis, and there is little room

for boasting or contempt. The schoolboy who
has mastered Cæsar despises his junior still struggling with the rudiments. But in the presence
of a ripe Latin scholar there is not so much
difference between the brothers after all. Just
so when a man sees little higher than himself, it
is tolerably easy to despise. But when the ideal
is lifted into the glory of Christ our superiority
has a strange trick of vanishing. It was the
Pharisee, whose standard of all things was the
Pharisee, who thanked God that he was not as
other men. But the poor publican, with his
God-touched conscience, and his vision of the
splendour and purity of heaven, could only cry,
' God be merciful to me the sinner.' With
such heights to scale, and with such depths to
loathe, it was impossible to despise the sorriest
brother. And every man who has been wakened
to the eternal has been wakened to the sight of
heights and depths like that. It is that heightening and deepening that comes through Christ
that robs a man of shallow self-content. And
to rob a man of shallow self-content is a sure
way to guard him from despising.

And then the gospel insists on human brotherhood. 'Our Father which art in heaven' is its prayer. Did the cultured Greek look down on the barbarian? Did the elect and covenanted Jew despise the Gentile? Did the free man look with an infinite disdain upon the slave? Clear as a trumpet, strong as the voice of God, there rang this message on a dying world : There is neither Jew nor Greek, barbarian, Scythian, bond nor free, but all are one in Christ. Yes, and when that word of command was obeyed, and the gospel of Jesus was carried to the heathen, and when the peace and hope and joy and comfort of it was offered in all its fulness to the slave, slowly, like a dark cloud, the contemptuous spirit of paganism scattered, and the star of brotherhood rose in the sky. It is our kinship in Christ, then, that is blotting out contempt. It is our brotherhood that has lightened that burden of despising. God meant us to be like that tiny lass in Edinburgh who was carrying a strapping infant in her arms, and when a stranger said, ' Why, what a burden for you,' she answered, ' Please, sir, he's no a burden, he's my brother.'

But the greatest power of all has still to be

named. It is the life and death of our Saviour
Jesus Christ. No man can struggle to be true
to that ideal, nor feel the love that brought Him
to the cross, but the contemptuous spirit we are
all so prone to will take to itself wings and fly
away. I ask you to trace the story of that life,
and tell me if you find a trace of despising there.
The fact is, Christ was despised for not despising :
the Jew could never understand His charity.
Did He despise the woman of Samaria though
all her village held her in contempt ? Did He
despise the publican, the harlot ? Did He ever
look with disdain on little children ? Christ saw
the worst as you have never seen it—felt all the
loathsomeness and guilt of sin—yet for the worst
all things were possible yet ; there was some chord
still capable of music. The sorriest sinner was
good enough to live for. The sorriest sinner
was good enough to die for. A man may be
poor, unsuccessful, vulgar, very dull ; but if he
can say 'Christ Jesus died for me,' I do not think
I shall despise that man again.

NEAR-CUTS NOT GOD'S

God led them not through the way of the land of the Philistines, although that was near.—Ex. xiii. 17.

It is strange to think that by the straight road it was a tolerably brief journey from Egypt to Palestine. Four or five days' hard marching, by the route that is now common with the traders, would have brought the children of Israel to the promised land. Four or five days would have done it comfortably; yet Israel took forty years to do it. And we know the hardships, and the sorrows, and the battlings, that filled with bitterness these forty years. Yet for all that, the leadership was God's. The pillar of cloud and fire led the advance. The longest way round was the shortest way home. There was a near-cut, certainly; but here, at any rate, the near-cut was not God's.

And it is not difficult to see with sufficient clearness some of God's reasons for this roundabout.

The Bible uplifts the veil a little, and we find first that there was compassion in it. That near way was through the land of the Philistines, and the Philistines were skilled and subtle in the arts of war. To have brought Israel face to face with *them*—Israel, fresh from the stubble-field, and with the broken spirit of the slave still in them—to have done that might have been to have spoiled everything, and to have sent them scattering and headlong back to Egypt. The time was coming when the armies of Israel would be more than a match for any ranks of Philistines. The time was coming—the Almighty was hastening it ; only the time for that had not come yet. So by a thousand lesser trials and combats, sharp brushes, unexpected difficulties, an all-compassionate God prepared the rabble to be a disciplined army of the Lord. And it took forty years to do that thoroughly. It was a very compassionate protraction. The road was very roundabout, granted. But it was the right road for all that.

But there was more than compassion in it ; there was education, and true compassion is generally educative. We hardly realise what we should have lost, nor how incalculably poorer the human race would have been, if Israel had been permitted the near-cut. Five days by the power of God might have brought them to Canaan, but still with Egypt and its bondage in their blood. It took one night to take Israel out of Egypt, but forty years to take Egypt out of Israel. And when I think of all that Israel learned, in the storm and the shadow of that devious journey ; when I remember how it enriched and deepened their knowledge of themselves, and of their God, I feel that the purpose of the Divine was in it : they were being educated for your sake and mine. God led them not through the way of the Philistines, though that was near. And we are all debtors to that leadership.

That, then, was one feature of God's guidance. It shunned the near road, and it took the roundabout ; and if you have been living with the open eye, and watching the method of the Divine in things, you have seen much that is analogous to this. But we forget so readily, that it is part of a preacher's office just to recall parallels at times. Let us name, then, some of the larger spheres, where again the near-cut was not God's.

Think of the discovery of nature's secrets : of coal, of iron, of steam, of electricity. God formed this world to be inhabited, said the prophet ; and these great powers, or instruments of power, have slumbered or flashed since the world was. And a single whisper from God would have communicated everything, and put mankind in possession of the secrets. Five days ?—five moments might have done it ; the world would have been at its Canaan, so to speak. But God never led us that way, though that way was near. There have been centuries of patient toil and striving ; endless mistake, long gropings in the dark ; there have been sufferings and sacrifices in the cause of science, as great as any of Israel in the desert ; and then, and not till then, at that long last, did the secrets of the world begin to dawn. It has been very roundabout, that road to power ; but it has been the right road, spite of its devious windings. For the powers of nature would have mastered us ; we should have been their slaves and not their lords had we been faced by them, just after Egypt. And in the efforts to know, to understand, and to see, we have learned so much, and have been so ennobled, that the roundabout has

been a priceless blessing, and we are all debtors
to that leadership.

Or rising upward, think of the coming of
Jesus. I detect the same leadership of God in
that. I see in it the action of that Hand that
took Israel to Canaan by a circuit. What is the
meaning of all the old religions? of the primitive
faiths that were old when Christ was born? And
what is the meaning of these thousand sacrifices
that smoked on the altar of Gentile and of Jew?
They mean that from the first dawn of history
man has been crying for a Saviour-God. Yet the
ages passed, and the Saviour never came. And
empires arose, and kingdoms passed away, and
philosophies were born and flowered and perished,
and the prophets prophesied and the psalmists
sung : and the world was dying, and all for want
of God. Surely, in response to the world's
need, He might have come a thousand years
before ! But God had no near way to Beth-
lehem. He led the world about ; and through
the desert, before He brought it to the king
at Nazareth. We see now that there was a
fulness of the time. There was kindness and
education on the road. The world had to be

led so to be ready, and we are all debtors to that
leadership.

There is one other region where a similar
guidance of God is very evident. I refer to the
evangelising of the world. We talk of the
difficulties men feel about foreign missions. I
believe that one of the greatest of them all, when
one seriously thinks about the matter, is the
slow progress that missions seem to make. After
the resurrection, on that glad summer morning,
men bowed to the gospel like a field of corn. And
Jesus Christ is still the power of God : why, then,
are the nations not yielding to His love ? Is there
no near road to the heathen ? No thrill from the
Infinite that might tingle through Africa till twice
ten thousand cried aloud for Jesus ? Ah, it would
be exquisitely pleasing ; but you must remember
near-cuts are not God's. Slowly, along the roads
that commerce has opened, and by the highways
along which battle marched, leaving them blood-
red in her own grim way ; slowly, by a man here,
and by a woman there, and the men not saints,
but of like passions with ourselves—and by
unceasing labour, and by unrecorded sacrifice, the
world is being led to know of Jesus. And we

have learned so much in that hard struggle, so much of the world, so much of human nature; we have seen such love evolved, such courage and such heroism, that we are all debtors to that leadership.

Now so far I have been dwelling on larger spheres; but I should be sorry ever to close a sermon without having a cast for individual souls. I wish to tell you, then, of one thing I have noticed in the Bible (and when a matter occurs often there, you may be sure there is need for such iteration), I have noticed that most of the high and generous souls—the gallant spirits of the two covenants, let me say—have been tempted with the temptation to take the near-cut, and in the power of God have conquered it.

Take Abraham, for instance. God had made a promise to Abraham that all the land of Canaan should be his. And Abraham dwelt in Canaan, and he grew rich in it, and he owned not a foot of it save his wife's grave. Do not you think he had counsellors in his tent, and in his bosom, to whisper to him, 'Abraham, arise! thou hast a host of followers; go out and win the land'? And Abraham could fight and conquer when he

liked—witness his battle with the five kings for
Lot's sake. But he refused that near-cut to the
promise; scorned it: said *God* must fulfil, not I;
and died in a strange country, dwelling in tents,
though God had pledged him Canaan for his own.
Tempted by the near road, he refused it. He felt
by faith that God's ways were roundabout. And
when he opened his eyes on the other side of Jordan,
and in the true Canaan saw the King in his beauty,
I warrant you he knew that God's road was best.

Or think of David. God had made a promise
to David, that the Kingdom of Israel would be
his. And David was persecuted and hunted in
the hills, till there came that never-to-be-forgotten
morning by the sheep-cotes, when Saul went into
the cave to cover his feet. And the men of David
said unto him, 'Behold the day of which the Lord
said unto thee: I will deliver thine enemy into
thine hand.' One stab, and his great enemy was
dead. The times were rough, and no one would
have blamed him. One *cut*—yes, a near-cut to
the throne. But 'the Lord forbid that I should
do this thing!' David refused it; put the thought
from him like poison. And when at last, after
Mount Gilboa, he came to his throne by the way

that God appointed, I warrant you he felt God's ways were best.

Or think with all reverence of Jesus Christ, tempted in all points like as we are, yet without sin. Why did He come to earth to live and die for us, but that the kingdoms of this world might become His? And the devil taketh Him up into an exceeding high mountain, and showeth Him all the kingdoms of the world, and saith to Him : 'All these things will I give Thee, if Thou wilt fall down and worship me.' It was the old temptation. I speak with utmost reverence—it was Jesus being tempted by near ways. There was a quicker and an easier road than Calvary. 'Ally Thyself, Jesus, in Thy magnificent powers —ally Thyself with the spirit of the world, and triumph is certain ; there need be no Gethsemane ; men will be quick to feel the King in Thee, and crown Thee.' Then saith Jesus unto him : 'Get thee hence, Satan, for it is written thou shalt worship the Lord thy God.' And when I think of the long road of Jesus, round by the villages, and through the Garden, and on to the cross, and into the grave, I feel, if I never felt it in my life before, that near-cuts are not God's.

Now I want you to carry out that doctrine.
You want to be prosperous? There is no near
road to that, consistent with Christian principle
and God. I often think of the gentleman who
said that the strongest temptation in his earlier
years was when the devil took him up into an
exceeding high mountain and showed him ten per
cent. And there is no near road to joy, nor to
Christian character ; you must go round by the
desert to that Canaan. Be patient. Do not be
showy, flashy. Hold to it, dourly, in the dark,
and go ahead. And though the way is strangely
roundabout, full of mistake and struggle and
secret cry, it will emerge, in the good time of God,
into the land that flows with milk and honey.

THE DEPARTING OF THE ANGEL

And they went out, and passed on through one street, and forthwith the angel departed from him.—Acts xii. 10.

In the verses that precede our text we have the familiar story of Peter's release from prison. Perhaps the story would have been still more familiar, and would have impressed itself still more vividly on Christendom, had it not been overshadowed by that other scene, when Paul and Silas sang in the gaol at Philippi. The world would have been a great deal poorer but for its prisons. We owe more to our prisons than we think. Shining virtues have been developed in them; miracles of heaven have been wrought in them; immortal literature has been written in them, and these are things we could ill do without. And we could not do without that word of Jesus either—Sick and in prison, and ye visited Me.

Peter, then, had been imprisoned by Herod.

He had been cast into the inmost ward. You can hear door after door shut-to behind him, with a re-echoing clang. And then, to make assurance doubly sure, he is chained to two soldiers as Paul was, afterwards, in Rome. Perhaps Herod thought that if Peter's Master, when He was left for dead, had burst from the sealed grave, it were well to make assurance doubly sure, when the prisoner was one of Jesus' henchmen. But there were some truths that Herod had yet to learn. And one of them was that when God Almighty works, 'stone walls do not a prison make, nor iron bars a cage.' Behold the angel of the Lord came upon Peter, and a light shined in the prison. You can shut out a man's nearest and dearest from him, but no authority can shut the angels out. And the angel touched Peter, and the chains fell off him. And the angel led him out from ward to ward. And the iron gate swung back upon its hinges, and Peter was out under the stars again. And the angel and Peter passed on through one street, we read, and forthwith the angel departed from him.

Now, do you see why the angel left the disciple then? There is strong doctrine in the departing

of the angel. Sometimes the angels leave us for
our sin. We are so coarse, and evil-inclined and
worldly, it would stain and sully their white robes
to walk with us. They try it for one street—for
we have all our chance ; but it does not prove ' the
street which is called Straight.' There is always a
dying out of vision when a man or woman loses
the childlike heart, and the dying of vision is the
departing angel. Sometimes, then, the angel leaves
the soul—the brightness fades, the heavenlies
disappear, the presence of white-robed purity is
lost—and all because a man is growing worldly.

But that was clearly not the case with Peter.
Right to the end, through all the struggle and
the storm of life, Peter preserved, as only the
greatest do, the great heart of a little child. If
every child has got its guardian angel, I do not
think that Simon's would be lacking. Yet for all
that, when they had passed through one street,
forthwith the angel departed from Simon Peter.
And I think it is not difficult to see why. The
angel's work was done ; that is the point. There
was no more need for the ministry of miracle.
Peter was a man among men now ; in the familiar
streets, freed from his shackles, and with friends

to go to—it was at that point the angel went
away. There was the presence of Christ for
Simon Peter now ; there was God in His eternal
law and love ; but there was no need for the
angel any more. His task was over when the
chains were snapt, and the last gate between Peter
and liberty swung wide.

I wonder if you grasp, then, what I should
venture to call the helpful doctrine of the departing angel ? I think it is a feature of God's
dealing that has been somewhat neglected in
our thought. It means that in extraordinary
difficulties we may reasonably look for extraordinary help. It means that when we are shut
in prison walls, and utterly helpless to extricate
ourselves, God has unusual powers in reserve,
that He is willing to dispatch to aid His own. But
when the clamant need goes, so does the angel.
In the open street, under the common sky, do
not expect miraculous intervention. It was better
for Peter's manhood, and it is better for yours, that
only the hour of the dungeon should bring that.
The angel departs, but the law of God abides.
The angel departs, but the love of Christ remains.
And I think that all God's leading of His people,

and all the experience of the Christian heart, might be summed up, with not a little gain, in the departing angel and the remaining Lord.

I want then to take that suggestion to-night and bring it to bear on various spheres of life. And first we shall think of Israel in the wilderness. There was a helplessness about Israel in the wilderness, like the helplessness of Peter in the prison. It was a terrible journey through that gloomy desert, twice terrible for these newly emancipated slaves. There were mighty barriers between them and Palestine quite as impassable as any prison-doors. They would all have perished but for angelic help. Hungry, the flight of quails came from the sea, and the ground was covered, in the red dawn, with manna. Thirsty, there flowed a stream of water from the rock, and they drank of the spiritual rock which followed them. The Red Sea became a highway for their feet, and they found a road right through the swellings of Jordan. It was the angel of God smiting their fetters off. It was the angel of God bursting the gates before them. Out of the dungeon and prison-house of Egypt they were carried by the constraint of irresistible power.

But then, when they reached Canaan and had, as it were, passed through one street of it, forthwith the angel departed from them. The manna ceased to fall after one harvest. They drank no more of the water from the rock. There came days when they were hunted down by enemies, yet the Jordan never stayed its flood again. Jehovah was with them still in love and law; the mystical presence of Jesus was their shield. But the need was past, the prison gates were broken, and they learned the doctrine of the departing angel.

Or we might think of the history of the Christian church in this light. We might compare Pentecost with after centuries. There was a radiance and a spiritual glory about Pentecost, that remind us at once of Peter and the angel. There were tongues, as it were of fire, on every head; the doors of that upper room were opened wide: the bonds of that little company were loosed; they were filled with joy, they got new gifts of speech. It was a season of wonder and of miracle; it was the intervention of heaven for an hour. And then the church passed on through one street mystical, and forthwith the angel

departed from them. Could Justin or Jerome or
Augustine work miracles? Does God give any
missionary *now* the gift of tongues? Can we
heal the lame with a word as Peter did? Can we
shake off the serpent as Paul did at Malta?
There are some men who would have us believe
we can ; and there are more who, knowing that
we cannot, think it impossible that it was ever
done. I beseech you to avoid these two mistakes.
Remember the doctrine of the departing angel.
We are out in the streets now, under the stars of
heaven ; miraculous ministries would simply ruin
our manhood. Once, when there were prison
gates to open, the angel came and gave the church
her liberty. But now the Lord is our shepherd
and our stay ; the grace of an abiding Christ
suffices. The angel has been summoned home to
God.

I think, too, that we become conscious of this
truth in the unfolding of our individual life.
There comes a time in the life of every one of us
when, not for our sin but for our deepest good,
the angel leaves us as he left Simon Peter. In
childhood we were very near the angels ; we
heard the beating of their wings sometimes, when

the world was hushed and everything was dark. We never thought of law or will or character ; we lived in a dreamland, and the great dream was God. ' Heaven lies about us in our infancy.' In my church in the far north—and a beautiful church it was—we had curtains on each side of the pulpit. The way into the pulpit was through the curtains. And I often used to notice a tiny girl gazing at these curtains with very eager eyes. It was quite clear it was not the minister she was looking at. It was whenever the curtains moved that she would start and stare. I found out afterwards what all the interest was. The little child thought that heaven was behind the curtains. It was only a wilderness of joists and planks ; but she thought that Christ was there, she thought that God was there ; she thought that the minister stepped out from God into the pulpit, and every time the curtain rustled—little heart, little eager, beating heart ! who could tell but thou mightst catch the shimmer of an angel there ? Ah, well, she has passed on through one street since then, and forthwith the angel has departed from her. She will never mistake an organ-loft for heaven again. She never expects to see the gleam of

wings now. And it may be that she looks back
half wistfully to the day of glory in the grass and
splendour in the flower. But my point is that
the angel must depart, if we are to walk the street
of life in our true dignity. We are not here to
dream that heaven is near us ; we are here so to
live that heaven shall be within us. And if at
every turn the angel met us, and the vision of a
dream enchanted us, we should lose heart and
nerve and power for the struggle, and be like the
lotos-eaters in ignoble quietude. The angel may
go, but duty still remains. The vision may
disappear, but truth abides. We never understand what *will* is, we never realise what we can
do, we never feel the worth of personality moved
by the spirit of an ascended Lord, till the hour
when the angel goes away. Therefore, in the
interests of highest and holiest manhood, we shall
thank God for the angel-atmosphere of childhood,
and thank Him none the less that when we have
passed through one street, forthwith the angel has
departed from us.

I think, too, and with this I close, I think we
may swing this thought like a lamp over the dark
chamber of the grave. In a great congregation

there are always mourners, and I do not like to close without a word for them. It may be there is some one here to-night who, looking backward, remembers an angel presence. Perhaps it was a mother, perhaps a sister ; but they were so gracious, so gentle, and so patient, that you see now it was of heaven, not of earth. And you thought it was going to be a lifelong comradeship ; you would travel on through all life's streets together. But you only passed on through one street, and forthwith the angel departed from you. And you are not yourself yet, any more than Simon was. The streets seem strangely unreal ; how the wind bites ! But like Peter when he came to himself, you too shall say, 'It was the Lord who sent His angel to deliver me.' There was some work to do, and it was done. There was some help to give, and it was given. There were chains to break and prison doors to open, and you can bear witness that it was all accomplished. Remember the doctrine of the departing angel, when the heart is empty and the grave is full.

UNDEVELOPED LIVES

Except a corn of wheat fall into the ground and die, it abideth
alone.—John xii. 24.

In this summer season, when the world is at its
fairest, one thing that impresses us very strongly
is what I might call the prodigality of nature.
Every flower is busy fashioning its seeds ; there
are trees with thousands of seed-vessels upon
them ; and we know that of all these millions of
seeds that are now forming, not one in ten
thousand will ever come to anything. Now, I
am not going to speak of the problems suggested
by that wastefulness : I have touched upon that
topic elsewhere.[1]   I wish rather to say a word or
two upon the subject of undeveloped lives.   In
every corn of wheat that finds no congenial soil,
there are undeveloped possibilities of harvest ;
and that suggests to me the question that often
vexes us, the question of undeveloped lives.

[1] 'Love's Wastefulness,' in *Flood-Tide.*

There are some seasons when we feel this more acutely. Allow me to recall some of these times to you. One is the hour when we are brought into contact with a strong and radiant personality. There is something very stimulating in such company, but often there is something strangely depressing too. Most of us have felt some sinking of the heart in the presence of exuberant vitality. I do not mean that we are repressed or chilled ; it is not the great souls, it is the little souls, that chill us. But I mean that the possibilities of life so overwhelm us, in the splendid outflow of a radiant nature, that we feel immediately, perhaps to the point of heart-sinking, how undeveloped our own life must be.

Again, we feel it in these rarer moments that come to us all sometimes, we know not how— moments when life ceases to be a tangle, and flashes up into a glorious unity. In such hours it is a joy to be alive ; thought is intense ; things quiver with significance. There is a passing expansion of every power and faculty, touched by mysterious influences we cannot gauge. I think that for Jesus every hour was like that. For us, such hours are like angels'

visits. But when they come they bring such
visions of the possible, that we feel bitterly how
poor are our common days. If this be our
measure we are not living to scale. If this be
our waking, is not our life a sleep? It is in the
rarer and loftier moments, then, that we apprehend
the meaning of undeveloped life.

But perhaps it is in the presence of early
death that the thought reaches us with its full
pressure. For the tragedy of early death is not
its suffering: it is the blighted promise and the
hope that is never crowned. I scarcely wonder
that in wellnigh every cemetery you shall see a
broken column as a monument. It is hardly
Christian, but it is very human, and I do not
think God will be hard on what is human. Wherever death is there you have mystery. But in
the death of the young the mystery is doubled.
And when there were high gifts of heart and
intellect the mystery is deepened a thousandfold.
Why all this promise? Why this noble overture? Why, when the pattern is just beginning
to show—

'Comes the blind fury with th' abhorred shears
And slits the thin-spun life'?

The great mystery of the early grave is the sorrow of undeveloped lives.

Now there is one thing that I should like to say in passing. It is that in the light of undeveloped lives there must be infinite pain in the omniscience of God. Do you remember how Robert Browning sang,

> ' All, I could never be
> All, men ignored in me
> *This*, I was worth to God ' ?

God recognises the value and the power of the possibilities we never even see. We take men as we find them, very largely. We do not trouble about latent powers. If our eyes were opened, in the city street, to the undeveloped love and gifts and character in the crowd, what a new sense of hopelessness would strike us! But the hungering of love we never dream of, and the craving of hearts, and the gifts that cannot blossom, all these are clear as a star to the Eternal, and that is one sorrow of divine omniscience.

Now one of the first things to arrest me in Christ Jesus is His influence in developing the lives He touched. It is as if God, in that sorrow of omniscience, had charged His son to call forth all possibilities. I doubt not there were other publicans with gifts as good as Matthew's, and other doctors quite as sincere as Luke ; but under the influence of Jesus Christ the gifts of these men so leapt into noble exercise, that they have made all Christendom their debtors, while the rest are sleeping in unrecorded graves. When Simon Peter first steps upon the scene he is a rash, impulsive, and impetuous man. One recognises the slumbering greatness of him ; but one feels the boundless possibilities of evil. But Jesus handles him and plays upon him as a master musician might play on his loved instrument, till the chords are wakened into such glorious music that the centuries are ringing with it still. *Nihil tetigit quod non ornavit :* Jesus touched nothing which He did not adorn. And He adorned, not as we decorate our streets, but as God adorns the lilies of the field. He drew from the worst their unsuspected best. He kindled the love and pity that were sleeping. He roused into most effectual exercise whatsoever gift or talent was concealed. And if to-day the aggregate life of Christendom is infinitely deeper,

fuller, and more complex, than any life the
world has ever known, we largely owe it to the
influence of Jesus in the development of human
life.

The question, then, which I desire to ask is
this : What were the forces that Jesus used in
this great work? And I wish you to notice,
as it were by way of preface, how the historical
career of Jesus makes the thought of development
independent of the years. We say that the days
of our years are threescore years and ten. We
get to think that threescore years are needed,
if human life is to come to its fruition. And
then we are confronted with the life of Jesus,
a life symmetrical, proportioned, perfect, and Jesus
of Nazareth died at thirty-three. Most lives
are just awaking into power then; but the life
of Jesus was perfect in its fulness. Most of us
would cry at thirty-three, 'It is beginning'; but
Jesus upon the cross cried, 'It is finished.' And
the great lesson which that carries for every one of
us is that we must not measure development by
time. There may be years in which every power
in us is stagnant. We live in a dull and most
mechanical way. Then comes an hour of call or

inspiration, and our whole being deepens and expands. A crushing sorrow, a crisis, or a joy, develops manhood with wonderful rapidity, and may do the work of a twelvemonth in a week. Let us remember, looking unto Jesus, and noting the shortness of that perfect life, that the scale of development is not the scale of years.

What, then, were the great forces Jesus used in developing undeveloped life? The first was His central truth that God is love. He taught men that in heaven was a Father; that the heart that fashioned them and ruled them, loved them; and in that vision of the love of God men found magnificent environment for growth. I think we all know how love develops character. I think most of us have known that in our homes. If in our childhood we were despised or hated, the most expensive schooling will not right things. A mother's love is the finest education. When a man is afraid he never shows his best. When all the faces around him are indifferent, there is no call upon his powers to stir. But when love comes, then all the deeps are opened, and life becomes doubly rich and doubly painful, and every hope is quickened, and every desire

enlarged, and common duties become royal
services, and common words take a new depth
of meaning. We all know how love develops
character. That was the first power that Jesus
used. He said to a repressed and fearful world,
'God loves you.' And if human life has been
developing in Christendom into amazing and
undreamed-of amplitude, it is primarily a response
to that appeal.

But there was another power that Jesus used.
It was the human instinct of self-surrender. It is
the glory of Jesus that He called self-surrender
into the service of our self-development.

There was one religion in the ancient world
that strove with all its power to make man
complete. It was the beautiful religion of the
Greeks, and its aim was to make life a thing of
beauty. It did not fail; but it slowly passed away.
It proved unequal to the terrible strain of life.
And one reason of its decadence was just this,
it had no place for the grandeur of self-sacrifice.
Then rose the noble philosophy of Stoicism, and
it grasped with both hands the truth of self-
surrender. It said the first duty of man is to
surrender, till he has steeled himself into impreg-

nable manhood. It failed, because life insisted on expansion. It failed, as every philosophy and creed must fail, that says to the God-touched soul, 'Thus far thou shalt come and no farther.' It had grasped the vital need of self-surrender, but by self-surrender it meant self-suppression.

And then came Jesus of Nazareth, Son of God. And He said, 'If thine eye offend thee, pluck it out.' Surrender thy sight, if need be; but then *why*? That the glories of heaven may break upon the soul. And if thou hast ten talents, give them out; and *why*? That thou mayst have thine own with usury. And if thou art a rich young ruler, sell all thou hast; and *why*? That thou mayst enter into the deeper, larger life, that comes from whole-hearted following of the Lord. The Greek had said, 'Develop and be happy.' The Stoic had said, 'Surrender and be strong.' But Jesus said, 'You never shall develop till you have learned the secret of surrendering.' I think, then, that that was Jesus' second power in advancing the development of life. He did not only say, 'Take up thy cross.' There were other teachers who might have said that too. But He said, 'Take up thy cross that

thou mayst follow *Me* '; and He is life abundant
and complete.

Lastly, and this is the crowning inspiration,
our Lord expanded life into eternity. Our life
shall go on developing for ever, under the
sunshine and in the love of God. 'I go to
prepare a place for you,' He said. The environment of heaven shall be perfect. Love is at
work making things ready for us that we may
ripen in the light for evermore. I know no
thought more depressing, as life advances, than
the thought that all effort is to be crushed at
death. It hangs like a weight of lead upon
the will, when a man would launch into some new
endeavour. But if death is an incident and not
an end, if every baffled striving shall be crowned,
if ' All, I could never be, All, men ignored in me,'
is to expand into actuality when I awake, I can
renew my struggle after every failure. It is that
knowledge, given us by Jesus, that has inspired
the development of Christendom. I affectionately
plead with you to make it yours.

THE SEARCH FOR HAPPINESS

Happy art thou, O Israel.—Deut. xxxiii. 29.

IT has often been noted that we bestow least thought upon our greatest blessings. We are hardly conscious of some of our greatest mercies, so long as God spares us the enjoyment of them. When a man is healthy, he thinks very little of health. He enjoys it, but he seldom dwells on it. And it is only when the day of pain arrives, or when the contrast between his own immunity and the sufferings of some neighbour grows accentuated, it is only then that a man truly wakens to the worth of the gift that has been his for years.

Now as it is with health, so is it with happiness. The happy man seldom thinks how happy he is. Other men see it ; perhaps feel a little envious. It is hard to be living in the mist and rain, when over the hill the sun is shining. But the heart that is happy is rarely introspective. There is a

childlike unconsciousness in its enjoyment. And
it is only when the happiness removes—when the
rose withers, when the sun is darkened—it is only
then that the mind appreciates the pricelessness of
what was held and lost. I think, then, that all the
world's talk of happiness is a proof that unhappiness is abroad. I think that in heaven, where
every one is happy, the question of happiness is
never raised at all. It is the unrest of life, it is
life's recurring agony, it is the shadow of it and
its pain, that make men eager when happiness is
mooted.

Now it is one of the strange contradictions of
our faith—and life and the universe are full of
such contradictions—that the gospel should have
proved itself, unquestionably, a powerful factor in
creating happiness ; and yet the central figure of
the gospel was a Man of sorrows and acquainted
with grief. The essence of Christianity—said the
great German poet—the essence of Christianity is
the worship of sorrow. And though that is false
in the sense in which he meant it, it is true that
sorrow lies bleeding at its centre. It cannot be
otherwise if Gethsemane is there. It cannot be
otherwise if the centre be the cross. Yet out of

that gospel, where grief seems to be crowned, has come, in the mystery of God, our happiness. Out of the cloud has come the call, Rejoice ! One of the powerful influences in history making for happiness, without a doubt has been the Christian faith. I wish then to note some gospel elements that have helped to make Christendom a little happier. I wish to show that faith in Jesus Christ is meant to give us what all the world's a-seeking.

First, then, it is commonly admitted that happiness is only gained as a by-product. I mean that if a man makes it the business of his life to extract happiness from any ore, he is almost certain to have his toil in vain. Let a man deliberately say, I will be happy : I am determined at every cost to lead a happy life ; the chances are he will be miserable. It is when we do *not* seek happiness that we find it. It is when we strive to overcome life's gloom, not by new pleasures, but by nobler interests ; it is when we aim at something higher than happiness, that happiness steals out and joins us on the road. Make it your all in all, it vanishes. Forget it, in the passion for sublimer things, it comes. That is one of the simple lessons of experience.

Now I want you to note that the gospel of
Jesus Christ deals with happiness along these very
lines. I have read the Bible from the first page
to the last, but I have never found that the chief
end of man was to be happy. There have been
philosophies which have made that their goal.
They have said that the first great end in life was
to enjoy. But that is so false to the dictates of
the heart, and to the sore-bought experience of
every traveller, that I do not marvel these philosophies died. The gospel of Jesus never says,
Be happy. The gospel does not deal in little
ironies. But the gospel of Jesus says, Be holy ;
aim at the highest and happiness will come.
Forget it ; trust in God ; do the next duty ; go
round by Calvary, if the road lies there ; and
like sweet music falling among the hills, or like a
fragrance wafted we know not whence ; like the
springing of water where we never looked for
it ; like the shaft of light breaking the cloud above
us ; like an angel unbidden, happiness will come.
Like its Lord, we shall find it when we sought
it not. Seek happiness first, says Jesus, and be
baffled. But seek ye first the kingdom of God,
and all these things shall be added unto you.

And it is because the gospel is true to the heart's teaching, carries it forward and gives the higher motive, that it is such a powerful ally in the search.

Once more, it has been commonly recognised that human happiness has two great enemies. No doubt it has a hundred enemies ; but there seem to be two who are its master-foes. What are they? Well, the one is Anxiety, and the other is Ennui or Listlessness. 'Anxiety and Ennui,' says a great writer,[1] in a book that is full of wisdom on the subject, 'are the Scylla and Charybdis on which the barque of human happiness is wrecked.' Are there not many in the church this evening who would be happy if they could slay anxiety ? Is it not to-morrow that is their sword of Damocles, hanging suspended over life's feast to-day? And surely we know, or at least we ought to know—it would make us less envious of the idle rich if we remembered it—that where there is no purpose in the life, no work to grip the rebellious days together ; then no wealth,

[1] This address was delivered on finding how many of our young men were absorbed in Professor Lecky's *Map of Life*. My indebtedness to that noble book, and my aim in so using it, will be at once apparent.

no luxury, no travel, no dissipation, can ever make the heart a happy one. 'Mount into your railways,' says Carlyle, in his own strong dramatic way, 'mount into your railways, and whirl from place to place at the rate of fifty, or if you like of five hundred miles an hour, you cannot escape from that inexorable, all-encircling ocean moan of ennui.' Anxiety, then, and Ennui—listless weariness—these are the Scylla and Charybdis of our happiness.

Now did it ever strike you that the gospel of Jesus is marvellously equipped to fight these foes? If there are two evils in the whole list of evils that the gospel can unhorse and hurl on to the sand, I think they are just Anxiety and Ennui. Anxiety? The very hairs of your head are numbered. Are not two sparrows sold for a farthing, and not one of them can fall without your Father? Cast thy burden on the Lord, He will sustain thee. The everlasting arms are underneath thee. Anxiety? Shame on our faithlessness! And ennui?—I cannot for the life of me conceive how any Christian can be a listless character. With a soul to save, and a character to build, with passions to master and virtues to achieve, with men to help and with a Christ to know, I think there is enough work for the idlest. That means, I take it, that the two great enemies of happiness have no such conqueror as Jesus Christ. It means that a living and true faith in Jesus helps men to what all the world's a-seeking.

But once again, it has been commonly admitted that happiness is to be found among life's common things. It is not the rare gifts, the possessions of the few ; it is not great wealth, great learning, great genius, or great power ; it is not *these* things that make the possessors happy. It is health, it is friendship, it is love at home ; it is the voices of children, it is sunshine. It is the blessings that are commonest, not those that are rarest ; it is the gifts that God has scattered everywhere. Professor Lecky speaks of a great writer who had devoted almost his whole life to one gigantic task. And at last, to his own surprise, his work was ended, and congratulations came pouring in on him from every side. Should he not have been supremely happy in that? Should he not have been thrilled with a strong sense of triumph? It was nothing, the writer said, nothing at all, compared with the joy he felt on hearing the approaching footsteps of some little children whom he had taught to love him. The greatest hour of his life, and the glory of it, could not make him so happy as the pattering footsteps.

And now comes in the gospel of Jesus, with its great power to consecrate the commonplace. For is it not the glory of Christ Jesus that He hath exalted them of low degree? It is not on the rare gifts that the gospel puts the emphasis. It is on the worth and power of lowly blessings. A Christian, as one has said, is not a man who does extraordinary things ; he is a man who does the ordinary things, but he does them in an extraordinary way. He brings the greatest to bear upon the least. He flashes on the very humblest task the light that never was on land or sea. He links his commonest joy on to the chain that runs right up to the throne of the eternal. In other words, the gospel gives added meaning to the very elements in life that make us happy. It lays its stress not on the rarities, but on the common blessings that are the source of happiness. And so emphasising them, so guarding and crowning them, it vastly increases the possibilities

of happiness, and helps men to what all the
world's a-seeking.

Lastly, I was much impressed by a word quoted
from a modern novelist ; and a true novelist
should know something of this matter, for it is
the distinctive genius of the novelist to interpret
the joys and sorrows of the heart. Well, one of
our modern novelists defines happiness thus :
'Happiness is a great love and much service.'
Love without service is a dream, a sentiment.
And service without love is taskwork always.
But happiness is a great love and much
service : that is the dictum of one who ought to
know.

Now the remarkable thing is that if any one
asked me to define Christianity, I think these are
the very words that I should use. If any one
said to me, 'What is Christianity—I mean what
is living and experienced Christianity ?' I should
answer, 'It is a great love and much service.'
For Christianity is more than love. It is love
militant, love going out to serve. And Christianity
is more than service. It is service rooted in the
love of Christ. Now I do not suppose that
the novelist was thinking of Christ when she

defined happiness so. She just wanted to tell what happiness was, and she stumbled on the gospel by mistake. Christ known, Christ loved, Christ served—yes! that is happiness. There is none other like it in the world.

CURIOSITY

And He smote the men of Bethshemesh because they had looked
into the ark of the Lord.—1 Sam. vi. 19.

IT was a great day for the men of Bethshemesh
when the kine came lowing along the highway,
and the ark of God was restored to them again.
It was like the restoration of nationality, when
they spied that symbol of God upon the cart.
The ark had been a prisoner with the Philistines.
Now it was back again, and there was hope.
I do not wonder that they rejoiced to see it, as
they were reaping their wheat harvest in the
valley.

But joy has got its perils as well as sorrow.
To be too glad is sometimes dangerous. The
heavens are all blue ; the only cloud on the
infinite expanse is but a speck no bigger than a
man's hand ; but elements of storm and thunder
may be in it. So was it at Bethshemesh as they
rejoiced while they were reaping their wheat

harvest in the valley. They were so happy, they forgot themselves ; something of reverence and awe had passed away. Here was the ark ; but were the old tables of stone inside the ark ? Or had the Philistines, with their impious hands, made havoc of that writing of God's finger? Oh how they longed to know ! Until at last, somewhat unhinged by joy, and it may be a little flushed with wine, their burning curiosity overmastered them, and they looked into the ark of the Lord. And God was angry at that rude impertinence, and He smote the men of Bethshemesh that they died. And the joy of harvest was turned into a dirge, because the Lord had smitten many of the people.

You see, then, what the sin of Bethshemesh was. It was the sin of unlawful curiosity. It was the irreverent prying of the thoughtless into the secret place of the Creator. Now do you think the circumstance exceptional ? A tale of some old and Oriental history ? O friend, although there are no golden cherubim with touching wings over the mercy-seat, although there are no staves to bear it by, no tables of grey stone from Sinai in it, remember there is still an ark of God ! There is an ark of God wherever man is, for the presence of the Infinite is there. There is an ark of God wherever Christ is, for in Him dwelleth the fulness of the Godhead bodily. And when I peer love-lessly into my neighbour's character, and when I gaze irreverently on the heart-mysteries of Immanuel, I do not know but that in the sight of God I am as guilty as Bethshemesh was.

Of course there is a curiosity which is lawful ; there is a curiosity which is really noble. We should never have reached our present heights of knowledge—the race would have been station-ary and stagnant—but for the fierce inquisitive-ness to know. Whenever I hear the questions of my child, I am carried back to the childhood of the race. And in the boundless curiosity of the raggedest bairn, I am near the secret of intellectual progress. And yet the noblest curiosity is seldom wholly and solely intellectual. It has roots in the heart ; it moves in a moral atmosphere ; it has visions of larger life and holier conduct. Far off, it does not culminate in self. It culminates and finds its crown in God.

A recent writer has illustrated this well, and
shown us this difference between lawful and unlawful curiosity, by distinguishing the two different
kinds of knowledge that a son may wish to
have of his father. One son might be intensely
curious to know his father's mind, his father's
heart. He is eager to learn what his father loves
and hates, that he may love what takes his father's
love, and hate the objects of his father's hate.
He wants to be like his father in his character.
That son is nobly and lawfully inquisitive. But
another son is curious to know what his father
is worth, and how much he will likely leave.
He wants to know if he can plunge into debt,
and if he can count on a life of pleasure
afterwards. And there is nothing moral,
nothing fine in that. It is a poor and worthless
curiosity.

Now which is your curiosity about God? That
is the question, children of the King! All idle
curiosity ends in self. It is myself, and my self-
love, it wants to gratify. But the curiosity that
is a moral power rests in the infinite providence
of God; prys not, for the mere sake of prying,
in the dark; believes that even in mystery is

good news ; then asks, and seeks, and knocks,
wherever God is, for it knows that love and life
and power are there. In other words, it is faith
that makes the difference. It is trust that deter-
mines the virtue or the sin. There is a kind
of curiosity that dies, the moment I trust my
brother or my God. It is not when I believe,
it is when I disbelieve, that I become imperti-
nently curious. Had Eve but trusted God with
all her heart, she had never been curious about
the fatal tree. Had the men of Bethshemesh
but trusted in Jehovah, and that He could guard
His own among the Philistines, they had never
been so curious about the ark. Had you and I
faith as a grain of mustard-seed, there would be
less impertinence abroad. O brother, we need a
deeper trust ; trust in the possibilities of every
man, trust in the intellect that plans and guides.
It is on *that* that the reverent, earnest curiosity
is built which carries a man to his noblest and
his best !

So necessary is this lawful curiosity, and so
useful for the enriching of humanity, that it is
quite clear to any fair observer that God is at great
pains to rouse it in us. It is one of the arts of

a loving and kindly God, to excite the curiosity
of His dull children.

Think of the world, for instance. Did it
ever occur to you how the wonderful beauty of
the world stirs a strange curiosity in the soul
about the Eternal ? It is the veiled figure in the
crowd that rouses interest, and the beauty of
nature is the veil of God. A man may be a
chemist or a scientist, and be so engrossed in
his particular study, that he never feels the
pressure of the infinite. But in the presence of
some glorious sunset, the noisiest chatterer grows
still a moment : it is as if it cried to him, 'Be
still, thou noisy one ; this splendour is the evening
garment of thy God.' So beauty, whatever other
ends it serves, helps to awaken the mystical in
man ; suggests far more than it can ever prove ;
hints that beyond the logic of the creed there is
something we cannot grasp and cannot utter. It
is the veil of the eternal figure. It keeps us
curious, eager, childlike till the end.

Or think of the great fact of personality. Is
not God at pains to make us lovingly curious
there ? There is not a soul but is wrapped in
strange disguises ; there is not a heart but is

veiled and hidden somehow ; all which, through
the ceaseless interactions of mankind, is one of
the ways of God to keep us curious. If I could
read my brother like a book ; if I could see into
his very depths ; if I could reckon him up, and
take his measure ; if there were nothing veiled
and hidden in him—I should never be curious
about my brother again. But in every man
there is an unexpected : something of mystery,
a veil, a problem ; and just because we have been
fashioned so, we are all and always of interest to
each other. It is that interest, degenerate and
corrupt, that makes the busybody and the scandal-
bearer. It is that same interest, touched by the
spirit of God, that breaks into sympathy and
brotherly kindness. Without it, we should all
be indifferent to each other.

Think of the Bible. Is there any book that
was ever given to man that stimulates curiosity
like that? It has been read, and studied, and
fed upon, and prayed through, for nineteen
centuries of growth and change, and the world
is curious about the Bible still. No man is
curious about the Shorter Catechism. The Con-
fession of Faith excites no curiosity. Yet the

truths of the Bible are gathered up in these, and they are a noble part of our inheritance. But the Bible is so simple, yet so deep ; so stern and majestic, yet so beautiful : it has the secret of such a sweet reserve ; it casts the veil of silence with such delicacy, and just at the point where we should give worlds for more ; that like the beauty of nature and the fact of character, it leaves us eager, stimulated, longing, curious. O restless, curious heart, be not discouraged ! That craving has been stirred by the Almighty. Do not degrade it. Consecrate it. Trust it. You shall be satisfied when you awake.

In closing, let me speak a word about Jesus' treatment of the curious spirit. And we cannot study the gospels without seeing—and it is very important that we see it—that Jesus was fully alive to the difference between lawful and un- lawful curiosity. When we remember how He hid Himself ; when we think that in every miracle there is some reserve, so that there is always ample room for curiosity, and no man is ab- solutely compelled to believe ; above all, when we recall the parables, and think how they sug- gested, stimulated, roused, and sent men home

to question and to wonder—we see at once that
Jesus recognised the place of curiosity as a religious force.

But then, on the other hand, remember this.
One day there came an idly-curious man to Jesus,
and he asked, 'Lord, are there few that be saved?'
And Jesus, turning to him sharply, said, 'Strive
ye to enter in at the strait gate.' And another
day, after He had risen from the grave, you
remember how Peter came, all curiosity, and said,
'Lord, and what shall this man do?' And Jesus
said to him, 'What is that to thee : follow thou
Me.' In both, the curiosity was idle. In both, it
was met in the same way by Christ. They were
recalled from questioning to quest. They were
brought back to action and to duty. There was
something for them to do—then let them do it.
The other matters may be left to God.

So when thou art tempted to be idly curious,
tempted to pry into forbidden things, I bid thee
remember that brief command of Jesus, 'What
is that to thee : follow thou Me.' Thou hast
a soul to save. Thou hast a life to sweeten.
Thou hast a cross to carry. Thou hast a heaven
to win. There is really no time to be nastily

inquisitive. Call home that utterly unworthy curiosity. Do your own work to your own music. And when this little sleep is over and we waken, we shall have such a long and steady look into the Ark, that we shall say it was worth waiting for.

SEEMING TO HAVE

From him shall be taken even that which he seemeth to have.—
Luke viii. 18.

You will observe that when our Lord speaks of
the man who seems to have, He is not referring
to the hypocrite. Our Lord poured out the vials
of His wrath upon the hypocrite, but it is not
the hypocrite who is in question here. There is
a sense in which every hypocrite seems to have.
He makes pretensions to virtues or to graces
that he does not in reality possess. But then he
is aware, more or less clearly, that he lacks them.
The hypocrite deceives others, not himself. But
this is a case of genuine self-deception. The man
is not practising trickery on anybody. There are
things that a man may imagine that he has, and
Jesus says he only seems to have them.

There are one or two notable instances of this
in the New Testament. For example, there is
the Pharisee in the parable. We quite mistake

the meaning of that parable if we think that the Pharisee was consciously a hypocrite. The moral of the story lay in this, that it was spoken to those who trusted in themselves that they were righteous. The Pharisee thanked God quite sincerely that he was a great deal better than his neighbour. He believed most genuinely in his superior self. There was no question in his own mind of his possessions. And the tragedy of the man's career is found in this, that he only seemed to have.

On a larger stage we are faced by the same spirit in the Church of Laodicea in the Apocalypse. It was a very prosperous and comfortable church. I am rich, it said. I am increased with goods, I have need of nothing. An exceedingly snug and smug society, with its own peculiar Laodicean smile. Yet thou art wretched, said the spirit of God ; and thou art miserable, and poor and blind and naked! The tragedy of that church's career is found in this, that it, too, only seemed to have.

I venture, then, to speak for a little this evening on that most subtle form of self-deceit. There is probably not one of us, in pew or pulpit, but is giving himself credit for what he does not possess.

Now, how is this? Can we detect the causes of this delusion? I shall endeavour to touch on some of them.

The first and the most innocent of all is inexperience. In all inexperience there is a seeming to have, which the rough and pushing world helps to dispel. I take it that every rightly constituted youth has a kind of lurking scorn for all his ancestors. All things are possible to faith, says the apostle. And all things are possible to one-and-twenty also. Unmatched with the intellect and power of the great world, untried by the searching discipline of life, we seem to have aptitudes, touches of heaven within us, that will carry us to the front imperiously. And then we are launched into the great deeps of life, and we find there were brave men before Agamemnon. It is a humbling and sobering experience. We have to recast everything, before we are through. But at least we come to know what we possess. We learn what we can do, and what we cannot. When we were immature and inexperienced, before we had come to grips with actuality—ah, then we *seemed* to have. To-day we have far less, but it is ours.

Again, this strange deception is intimately connected with self-love. We seem to have much that we do not really have, simply because we love ourselves so well. In all love, even the very purest, there is a subtle and most exquisite flattery. Love is not worthy of its name at all, unless it clothes its object with a thousand graces. You who are fathers and you who are mothers here —you don't know how much you seem to have to your young children. It is enough to make the hardest of us cry to God for mercy when we remember that, to our child of five, we are still perfect. You know the kind of week you spent last week ; yet to your little family there is not a stain on you. Such love is wonderful, passing the love of women. And was there ever a mother who was not quite convinced that her one-year-old was a most marvellous child ? He seems to have, because she loves him so. I think you see, then, the point I wish to make. Love can make any wilderness blossom as the rose. And never a child loved the most honoured father, and never a mother loved the dearest child, more passionately than most men love themselves. It is thus that to the end we *seem* to have, just because self-love is dominant. It is thus that he that hateth his life for Christ's sake begins to learn the secret of self-knowledge.

Often, again, we imagine we possess, because of the pressure of the general life around us. We move in certain circles of society ; we are surrounded by what we call public opinion ; and by the pressure of our environment upon us, our life takes its colour and its trend. Now I am far from saying that these outward influences may not have a very real effect on a man's character. Some of the most useful habits we can form may be formed through compliance with social convention. But there is always the danger of mistaking for our own the support we get from the society we move in. And it is only when that external pressure is removed that we discover how we only seemed to have. Put any man of average sensibility into the company of born enthusiasts, and in a week's time you shall have him enthusiastic. There are hours when the dullest talker feels that he is getting on excellently in conversation, and it is not till afterwards that it begins to dawn on him that some one else had the magnetic charm. We seem to have, we think that we possess ; but the possession is not really ours. Here is a man living at home in Scotland, a man of correct, perhaps exemplary conduct. He is a regular churchgoer at home ; he is quite interested in church affairs. But he goes abroad to China or to India, and there is little of the old Scottish feeling round him now ; and gradually, almost insensibly, he drifts away from the old reverence, till the kindliest critic dare not call him religious. What I want you to note is that that man was not a hypocrite. He was not consciously deceiving anybody when he lived that exemplary life at home. He never possessed his possessions, that was all. He was guided and moulded by an outward pressure. He seemed to have the root of the matter in himself, and it lay in his surroundings all the time.

Now our Lord tells us the fate of these fancied possessions. From him shall be taken even that which he seemeth to have. Sooner or later, as our life advances, we shall have our eyes opened to these fond delusions. We are to be so led, each one of us, that there will be no mistaking what is really ours. I want to ask, then, what

are God's commoner methods for making clear to
us what we only seem to have.

One of the commonest of them all is action.
We learn what we possess by what we do.
There are powers within each of us waiting to be
developed ; there are dreams within each of us
waiting to be dispelled, and it is by going forward
in the strength of God that we learn our limita-
tion and our gift. I am sure there is not one
man in middle life here but has been surprised
by the revelations of his past. He has been
called to work he never dreamed of doing ; his
way has led him far differently from his wish.
There were gifts which you were quite certain
that you had ; but the years have gone, and you
are not so certain now. Meantime, out of the
depths of self, some unsuspected powers have
been emerging, and the hand that has quickened
them into life is duty. The men who do nothing,
always seem to have. So-and-so is a genius, we
say ; if he would only exert himself, what he might
do ! Well, probably he would cease to be called
a genius if he did, and, therefore, he is wise in
doing nothing. I do not call that genius. I call it
cowardice. Life is given us just to find out what

we can do.   And it is through a thousand tryings
and a thousand failures that we come to find
what is really our own.   That is one of the great
gains of earnest duty.   We learn from it the
confines of our kingdom.   It is by action that
there is taken from us that which we only seem
to have.

This, too, is one great gain of life's variety.
It shows us what is really our own.   We are
tested on every side as life proceeds, and every
mood and change and tear is needed, if we are to
be wakened to what we seem to have.   It is so
easy to be patient when there is no worry.   When
there is no peril, it is so easy to be brave.   It is
when the whirligig of time brings its revenges
that we discover more exactly what we own.   If
I want to know the value of an army, I must wait
till the campaign has tested it.   It may seem to
be perfectly equipped for service, yet a month on
the field may teach us other things.   So you and
I, seeming to have so much, are marched into
battle, led over weary miles ; we are kept waiting,
we are baffled, wounded ; till out of all that
changeful discipline, that which we seemed to have
is taken from us.   One of the functions of our

vicissitudes is to strip us bare of what we seemed
to have. Life is so ordered for us in its heights
and depths, its changes, its hopes, its sufferings,
its fears, that, unless we are blind, we shall discover gradually all that is ours and all that only
seems so.

And if life fails, remember death is left.
Death is the great touchstone of the man. We
may be self-deceived for threescore years and ten,
but the deception ceases on the other side. There
we shall know even as we are known. Know
what? Among other things, ourselves. There
will be no delusions concerning our possessions
when our eyes open on that eternal dawn. I bid
you remember there will be no seeming to have,
before the great white throne and Him who sits
on it. All that is accidental and imaginary will
be revealed in the light of that great day. If we
have never let action do its work, and never seen
ourselves amid life's changes, we have not escaped
the judgment of the Christ.

I have sometimes thought, too, and with this I
close, that the words might apply even to those
we love. Is it not true, in the realm of the
affections, that sometimes we have and some-

times we seem to have? We are thrown into
close relationship with others ; we are bound to
them with this tie and with that. We call them
friends ; we think we love them, perhaps. Is it
real, or is it only seeming? Nothing can tell
that but the strain of life, and the testing of friendship through its lights and shadows. Nothing
can tell that finally but death. All that seemed
love, and was not really love ; all that we fancied
or mistook for friendship ; all *that* is taken from
us, passes away, in the hour and the separation of
the grave. But true affection is an immortal
thing ; nothing can separate us from love indeed.
Where hearts unite, there is eternity. And in
eternity partings are unknown.

A PLEA FOR SIMPLICITY

The simplicity that is in Christ.—2 Cor. xi. 3.

THERE are some words that have a tragic history. To the hearing ear and to the understanding heart they whisper strange secrets about human progress. If we could follow them through all their changing meanings we should be reading the story of mankind. Nor, indeed, when we think of it, is this to be wondered at. For language is the echo of the soul. And whenever the soul of man has struggled heavenward I shall hear its echo high among the hills. The man who thoroughly knew the English tongue could almost sit down and write an English history. It is because we now rise and now fall that words become ennobled or debased.

Now one of the words that has a pitiful history is that word simple. It has wandered far from the simplicity of Christ. It has so changed its dress, and lost its early character, that we are

almost ashamed to keep it company. Once, to
be simple meant to be free from guile. Simplicity was the opposite of duplicity. But in the
struggle with the world's sharp wits the guileless
man has generally fared so badly, that the simple
man has become the simpleton. I warrant you
there was a world of holy meaning in the word
innocent, when Adam and Eve first felt the taint
of sin. Yet now we look at the idiot, and we
pity him, and we say, 'He is an innocent.' So
once to be simple meant to be a Nathanael. And
now it almost means to be a fool.

And yet, if we have ever studied history at all,
we must have been struck with a certain sweet
simplicity about the characters of the very greatest
men. There is something of the child about the
greatest; a certain freshness, a kind of sweet
unconsciousness; a happy taking of themselves
on trust; a sort of play-element throughout the
drama. And all the time, powerfully, perhaps
silently, they were swaying and steering this poor
tossed world. Did you never feel that simplicity
in Martin Luther? And did it never arrest you
in George Washington? And did you never
mark it in the great Duke of Wellington? One

of the finest odes Tennyson ever wrote was his
ode upon the death of that great duke. And I
know not if in all the noble verse of it, it rises
to anything loftier than this :—

> Foremost captain of his time,
> Rich in saving common-sense,
> And, as the greatest only are,
> In his simplicity sublime.

The greatest souls, then, have been truly simple.
It is that simple element that has charmed the
world. And I cannot think of any better witness
to the abiding charm of true simplicity, than the
way in which vice has always tried to imitate it.
Make up your mind clearly on this point: that
sin is never simple, it is subtle. You may reject
the story of Eden if you will, but the insinuating
serpent is still sin. All sin is subtle, intricate,
involved ; leading a man into an infinite maze.
It can give a hundred reasons for its counsel,
when a good conscience is content with one. Do
you remember how the great poet of Germany in
his immortal tragedy of *Faust*—do you remember
how he pictures Mephistopheles as the master of
a consummate subtilty? He is always changing,
that evil incarnation. He is always compliant :

he is never the same. To Margaret he is one
thing, and to Faust another. He is exquisitely
accommodating everywhere—until we feel afresh
how subtle sin is, what an utter stranger to
genuine simplicity ! And when sin shams that
it is very simple—and it is very fond of that
device—we learn how attractive simplicity must
be. It is a well-known practice of the hypocrite
to make believe he is unusually candid. One of
the last arts of an abandoned woman is to act
like an innocent young girl again. It is the
unwilling tribute of the bad to that simplicity
of soul that charms the world, but which is lost
when the eye ceases to be single, and when the
conscience ceases to be true.

Now the most casual student of the life of
Jesus must have noted the simplicity of Christ.
In a sense far deeper than any other captain, our
Lord is in His simplicity sublime. His name
shall be called Wonderful, it is quite true. He
was the Counsellor, the everlasting King. But
He was holy, harmless, undefiled ; and a little
child shall lead them, said the prophet.

Think of His mode of life : was it not simple ?
It puts our artificial lives to shame. There is a

music in it, not like the music of the orchestra,
but like the music of the brook under the trees.
He loved John and Peter, not the Pharisee ; and
He drew to the children, not to the scribe ; and
it was all so natural and simple, that the blind
Jews said, this is not the Christ.   Had He come
greatly, with some sound of trumpet, they would
have hailed Him and cried, Behold ! Messiah
cometh.   But they missed the divinity of what
was simple, and He came unto His own and
they received Him not.

Think of His teaching : was not that simple
too ?   It puts our sermons and our books to
shame.   There is a false simplicity that springs
from lack of thought—and there is a spurious
and forced simplicity that I have heard some
ministers adopt when they began, with a smile,
to preach to the children—and how the children
hate it !   But true simplicity is the first-born
child of earnestness ; and of a deep and certain
knowledge of the theme ; and it was that, irradiated with divine compassion, which inspired the
simplicity of Christ the teacher.   Some cynic once
said a very bitter thing about the style of Gibbon
the historian.   He said that the style of Gibbon

was a style in which it was impossible to tell the
truth. With the deepest reverence for our
ascended Lord, I should venture to say just the
opposite of Him—the style of Jesus the Teacher
was a style in which it was impossible to tell a lie.
It was so clear, so pure, so exquisitely truthful.
It was so urgent in its invitation. It was so
sharp and straight in its rebuke. It rang so true
to their own village accent, and was so fragrant
with the sweet scent of their own hills, that men
did not realise in that simplicity the wisdom and
power of the Eternal God.

But the simplicity of Christ comes to its crown
in the feast of the Lord's Supper. There is no
gorgeous rite or showy ceremonial. There is
nothing of that many-coloured pageantry that
had once been needful to attract the world.
A cup of wine and a piece of broken bread—
these are the seals and symbols of the gospel.
And I never feel the simplicity of God and of
God's great plan for rescuing the world—I never
feel it so powerfully and so freshly as when I
sit at the Communion Table. There are great
mysteries in our Redemption. There are deep
things that even the angels cannot fathom. But

in the centre is a fact so simple that its best ritual is bread and wine.

Indeed that very simplicity, I take it, is part of the offence of the Cross. For such a complicated curse as self we should dearly love a complicated cure. We are like Naaman, the leprous captain of Assyria, who came to Israel to be cured of leprosy. And Naaman was mightily vexed and indignant when he was told to wash in Jordan seven times. I recall how M'Crie in his great *Life of Knox*—and a recent historian has said about that book that the man who has studied the period most deeply will feel most deeply how much he owes to it—well, M'Crie in his *Life of Knox* mentions among the things that hindered the progress of the Reformation, the great simplicity of the pure gospel. There was something fascinating to the youthful mind in the intricate subtleties of mediæval logic. There was a certain appeal for them in that vast rambling structure, that had been built by the schoolmen and called theology. And when the evangel came with its glad news of pardon, and out of the mists and chaos of the ages stept Jesus with the dew of His youth still on His brow, it was all so simple that

they took offence. O friend, do not thou take
offence ! Remember that ours is a universal
gospel. It has been preached this summer
Sunday by the grave of Livingstone. It has
been sung in the villages of India. It has been
spoken beside the Tigris and Euphrates. It was
declared to-day in the Pacific Islands. It has
cheered the sick, it has comforted the dying, it
has done that, and a thousand times more, this
summer day—and you do not want an intricate
gospel to do that. I have a Saviour who looked
on life as life ; and never thought of it as some
quiet academy. I have a gospel that in its great
simplicity is level with the strain of life and
death. It is worth preaching. It is worth be-
lieving. An intricate faith in such a world is
self-condemned. The Cross is, as the greatest
only are, in its simplicity sublime.

I want you all then to feel again, still more I
want you all to practise, the true simplicity that
is in Jesus Christ. And what we need is a little
more faith in God ; a little more independence
of the world ; a little more trust in an indwelling
Holy Ghost, and the separate guidance He is
giving to each. One of the foremost of our living

critics says a beautiful thing about the songs of
Shakespeare—the songs that we find scattered
through his plays.   He says that the songs of
Shakespeare are the only perfectly simple songs
in English, and they are that because of Shakespeare's faith.   Other men halted, hesitated, and
were afraid.   They said, ' *That* will look foolish,
and what will men think of *this* ? ' until the touch
of simplicity was gone.   But Shakespeare, thinking of no man, sang like a bird ; trusted his
genius, and was very simple.   And so I want
you to trust your God.   And if we hold to
it, quietly, without fret, that it is always better
to be good than bad, that it is always better
to be pure than impure, that duty is duty,
that conscience is supreme, that God is living,
that Jesus died for us ; then, spite of all the
genius of Shakespeare, our song, our life-lilt, our
music of the soul, may come to be just as simple
as was his.

'AFTER THAT, THE DARK'

He knoweth what is in the darkness.—Dan. ii. 22.

THESE words occur in a prayer of thanksgiving uttered by Daniel, and we must remember the strange circumstances that had moved the prophet to this prayer. Nebuchadnezzar had dreamed a dream : it had troubled his spirit till he started up, awake. In the language of Scripture, his sleep brake from him 'even as a bird out of the fowler's snare.' But when the king woke his dream had vanished from him. He could not recall it; it was quite gone from memory. There only remained the haunting consciousness that something portentous had loomed up in sleep. So the king called for the magicians of his court. They must tell him his dream; they must find out what he dreamed of ; they must declare not only the interpretation, but the matter and substance of the vision as well. It is little wonder the Chaldeans answered, 'There is not a man on earth that can show the king's matter.' Then

Daniel heard the command of Nebuchadnezzar.
And he went apart with his three friends, and they
prayed about it. He pled with God to tell him
what the dream was, and God was graciously
pleased to hear His child. Then was the secret
revealed to Daniel in a night-vision, and Daniel
blessed the God of heaven. Blessed be the name
of God for ever and ever, said Daniel, for wisdom
and might are His. He giveth wisdom to the
wise, and knowledge to them that know understanding. He revealeth the deep and secret
things. He knoweth what is in the darkness.

Now when the Bible tells us that God knows
a thing, we have to widen the thought of knowledge a great deal. So much of our knowledge is
merely speculative, not vitally linked with life
and character, that we are apt to forget that
all God's thought and love really lie latent in
what He knows. Sometimes when we have done
anything unworthy the vision of a good woman
comes before us, and we say in our hearts, or
perhaps we say to our neighbour, 'I would not for
worlds that she should know it.' We mean that
there are some men and women whom we might
tell it to, and the knowledge would make little

difference to them. But there is one so sensitive, so true, so good, that to know it would wound her to the very heart. It is a great thing to have a friend like that. Now something like that, only infinitely higher, should be in our minds whenever we say 'God knows.' There is thought, love, wisdom, preparation, action, in the bosom of the knowledge of the Eternal. He knoweth our frame : that means that He will pity us. He knoweth the way that I take : that means that He will guide me. He knoweth what is in the darkness : then He will use it for Daniel, whom He loves.

Now I want to take this great thought of our text and run it out along three lines to-night. Firstly, He knoweth what is in the darkness of the heart. Secondly, He knoweth what is in the darkness of the lot. And thirdly, He knoweth what is in the darkness of the future.

First, then, He knoweth what is in the darkness of the heart.

There is a well-known passage in that gentle and wise book, *The Autocrat of the Breakfast-Table*, in which the autocrat startles the breakfast-table

by a remark on two men in conversation. He
says that whenever two men are engaged in conversation, there are really six men present and not
two. There is the man as his friend pictures him
to be. There is the man as he pictures himself
to be. And thirdly—though the writer puts it
first—there is the real man, known only to his
Maker. The other men in each case are ideal.
Self-love touches up the picture, or the love of
friendship puts a halo round it. But the man
as he is in himself—the real man—that man is
known only to his Maker : He knoweth what is
in the darkness.

And the more we study that strange problem
of self, the more we feel that Dr. Holmes is
right. In the most ordinary life are deeps you
cannot fathom. In your own heart is a darkness
that you never penetrated. If we could only see
into the gloom as God sees, we should not surprise
each other as we do. Who knows what dreams
are thronging in the brain when the fingers are
busy with the daily work ? Who knows what
unrest, dissatisfaction, craving are cloaked and
masked by that sweet face ? Who knows what
suggestions of evil may have risen even in this

sanctuary where God is present to-night ? We
are all far more mysterious than we know. The
roots of our best and our worst are in the darkness. It is *that* that makes a man lean hard on
God, and say He knows what is in the darkness.
In that vast world which is beneath our consciousness, where life has its spring and the desires are
born, where far beneath our touch or sight are the
primary impulses that shall determine everything,
it is *there* that prayer and faith and trust work
miracles, for they are our appeal to the only
Being in the universe who knoweth what is in the
dark.

Now no man can doubt God's knowledge of
that realm, who will seriously read the life of
Jesus Christ. Few things arrest us more in that
high story than how Jesus explained men and
women to themselves. I don't think you and I
would have given our best to that poor and half-
wrecked woman of Samaria. I don't think you
and I would ever have dreamed of finding a
magnificent apostle in Simon Peter. But Jesus
Christ knew what was in the darkness, and twenty
centuries have justified His choice. Why, too,
when they asked Him one thing, would He some-

times answer as it were another thing? Why did
He say about Herod, 'Go tell that fox'; or to
the crowd that was gathered round the woman,
'Let him that is without sin throw the first stone
at her'? It was Christ finding His way into the
gloom. It was the Son of God touching the
secret soul. It was the witness and proof, upon
the stage of history, that He knoweth what is in
the darkness of the heart.

This thought has a twofold bearing upon
practice. It is, first, a great comfort when we
are misunderstood. I am not speaking so much
of great misunderstandings; it is a man's duty to
get these explained at once. Lives have been
ruined through great misunderstandings, hearts
have been made unutterably miserable, when half
an hour, face to face and eye to eye—and the
birds would have been singing in the trees again.
But apart from these there are the lesser misunderstandings, that fret a man's spirit every day he
lives. The things we try to do, and do so badly;
the kindnesses we mismanage so wofully; the
words we would fain speak and sometimes cannot.
The fact is that all expression is clumsy; we
cannot adjust it to the spiritual movement; we

grope and stumble to explain ourselves, and perhaps we are never really understood. And it is
then that, with a sense of restful comfort, we
remember He knoweth what is in the darkness. Do you recall how Dr. Newman put that
thought?

> ' Time was I shrank from what was right
> From fear of what was wrong.
> I would not brave the sacred fight
> Because the foe was strong.
>
> But now I cast that finer sense
> And sorer shame aside,
> Such dread of sin was indolence,
> Such aim at heaven was pride.
>
> So when my Saviour calls, I rise
> And calmly do my best,
> Leaving to Him with silent eyes
> Of hope and fear, the rest.
>
> I step, I mount where He has led,
> Men count my haltings o'er.
> I know them ; yet tho' self I dread,
> I love His precept more.'

But the thought is more than a comfort when
we are misunderstood. It is a caution against
judging others. I think we would be very loth
to judge a man if we only remembered that
doctrine of the text. Tennyson makes Merlin

speak ' of that foul bird of rapine whose whole prey is man's good name,' and nothing is more amazing than the recklessness with which we pass judgment upon a brother's action. I want you to remember that behind every action there is a darkness into which no one sees but God. I want you to remember that for the simplest deed, motives are intricate, involved, entangled. I want you to feel that unless you unravel motive, the judgment is bound to be inadequate. It is always wiser, and it is always kinder, to regard judgment as the prerogative of Heaven. Judge not that ye be not judged. You do not know—He knows—what is in the darkness of the heart.

Secondly : He knoweth what is in the darkness of the lot.

There are two words that sum up the trials of human life. The one is shadow and the other is cross. The one suggests the thought of darkness; the other hints at the burdens we must bear. I sometimes think we should handle our lives better if we learned to distinguish the shadow from the cross. Christ says to every disciple, ' Take up thy cross '; but no man would dream of taking up a shadow. We walk into it as bravely as we may, and by and by we shall reach the other border. We are prone to say, ' What a dark shadow this is,' when it is really a cross given us by God to carry. And sometimes we say, ' This is a heavy cross,' when it is only a shadow we shall leave to-morrow morning. Learn to distinguish, to separate a little. ' Divide and conquer' holds in the spirit world. The darkness of life is dark enough, God knows, without the added darkness of confusion.

Now if there is one thing on earth that is hard to understand, it is the meaning and the content of life's darkness. It has been the stumbling-block to countless feet ; it has tried the faith of innumerable hearts. The world has been asking what is the meaning of pain, and what is the meaning of trial and of tragedy, ever since man began to ask at all ; but when trial and sorrow knock at your own door, the answers of all the ages shall not satisfy. There is an element of surprise in all affliction. There is something different from all we ever heard of. If every joy is different from every other joy, every separate sorrow is a new thing too. Darkness may have enwrapped ten thousand hearts, but in *our* darkness somehow we stand alone. And then we crave to understand the thing. We do not want sympathy, so much as explanation. We want to know the content of that darkness, and we come home from the world saying, ' The world does not know.' And it is then, finding that flesh is vain, and turning full-faced to the Eternal God, we hear the exquisite music of our text, ' He knoweth what is in the darkness.' He knoweth, and His name is Love. He knoweth, and He so loved the world that He gave His only begotten Son to die for us. He knoweth, and we are His ignorant children, but by and by we shall know as we are known. There is a Christian agnosticism and a Christian stoicism that find their charter in this noble text. Until the day break, and the shadows flee away, it is enough that He knoweth what is in the darkness.

And is not all that exemplified most powerfully in the sufferings of our Saviour Jesus Christ? I think that Jesus in His agony in the Garden is the loneliest figure in all history. Peter and James were there, and John was there ; and Peter and James and John loved Jesus fervently.

But they all slept, they could not watch one hour;
they never guessed what was in the darkness. And
the other nine knew nothing of it all, and the
children in every cottage were asleep. None
knew but God, the Eternal God in glory, stooping
in infinite pity to the earth—none but the Father
knew what was in the darkness when the bloody
sweat dropped, and the hands were pierced. All
Christendom knows now; for it has saved us.
That blood speaks better things than that of Abel.
In the darkness of Christ's lot there was untold
treasure. Who knows how it shall be with you
and me?

Thirdly, and lastly: He knoweth what is in the
darkness of the future.

I think we are all agreed that it is a very
merciful provision that God has hidden the
to-morrow from us. I think we all feel that it
is infinite kindness that has hung that veil over the
coming days. Did you ever think how life's
novelty would go, and how the zest and charm of
it would pass, if we could see every to-morrow
perfectly? Even in the best company a road
grows weary, when we see the levels for long

miles ahead. I fancy, too, there have been hours
for most of us of such unutterable strain and
agony, that had we foreseen them ten years before,
we should have given up life's battle altogether.
I do not wonder that the great prophets of Israel
were men bowed under a certain noble melan-
choly. The bravest hearts could not escape that
shadow, if God revealed to them things of the
future. And who can tell how the sufferings of
Christ were deepened—touched to an intensity we
cannot conceive—by His knowledge of the cross
that was in store !

Of course, to a certain limited extent, we *do* see
into the darkness of to-morrow. We live in a
world of most inflexible law, and as a man soweth
so also shall he reap. They say that in the con-
volutions of the acorn the microscope sees all the
promise of the oak ; and in the bosom of a man's
to-day, with its struggle and conquest, or idleness
and waste, it takes no prophet to discern to-
morrow. The pity of the ill-regulated hour is
that the hours yet to strike shall feel its pressure.
The joy of an earnest morning is just this, that it
shall be easier to be earnest when a new morning
dawns. If we could separate life into isolated

seasons, the task of living would be infinitely simpler. It is the fact that every hour lives on, to influence every other hour, that makes the joys of life so stern and glorious, and the failures of life so exquisitely sad. To a certain extent, then, and in the moral sphere, each of us *does* see what is in the darkness. We are fellow-workers with God, and share His vision.

But after all it is a limited vision. It is only one little corner of the veil that is removed. The fact remains that in His infinite pity we are shielded and safeguarded by our ignorance; and the quiet thinker will waken every morning saying to his own heart, 'God knows.' It is one great secret of a well-spent life to live not by the year or by the month, but by the day. And the secret of *that* secret is to trust that God, who is Love, knows what is in the darkness. Is there a father here anxious about his son? Is there a mother who cannot bend over her little children but the thought of coming years hurts like a pain? Am I speaking to any man this evening, present perhaps for the first time in this church, who would give himself to God wholeheartedly but for the haunting dread of after days? Is there any one nerveless and worried so that he cannot worship, cannot be happy at home, perhaps cannot sleep? My brother or sister, 'God is love, and He knoweth what is in the darkness.' The secret of strength and quietness is there.

COUNTING THE COST

For which of you, intending to build a tower, sitteth not down first and counteth the cost, whether he have sufficient to finish it ?

Lest haply, after he hath laid the foundation, and is not able to finish it, all that behold it begin to mock him,

Saying, This man began to build, and was not able to finish.

Or what king, going to make war against another king, sitteth not down first, and consulteth, whether he be able with ten thousand to meet him that cometh against him with twenty thousand ?

Luke xiv. 28-31.

It is notable that in these two little parables, which deal with the great endeavours of the human soul, our Lord brings in the figure of the builder, and of a king making war upon another king. Christ always took human life at its best and kingliest, and even his illustrations have a royal touch. But the point to note is that Christ compared life to building. Life was like architecture or like war. Building and battling—these are the Master's figures ; and I do not think the world has ever bettered them.

There are rare souls that seem to grow, not build. And it may be some of us have known one saint—our mother perhaps—who bore no marks of conflict anywhere, and seemed to have reached the highest without a struggle. But for most of us it is the other way. Effort on effort, failure after failure, we have to forge and hammer ourselves towards what is honourable. And there are days when we seem to be building up a prison-house, until God in His mercy shatters that to fragments. Just note, then, that it is in a little parable of building that our Saviour teaches us to count the cost.

Now, any one who has read much in religious literature must have been struck by a kind of contradiction in it. He must have been arrested by two opposite conceptions of what religion really demands. I read some sermons, or I listen to some preaching, and religion seems exquisitely sweet and easy. I thought there was a cross in our religion, but when I read some of our current literature—if there be a cross it is so wreathed with honeysuckle that a poor soul can stumble past it easily. The valley of the shadow seems to have grown antiquated ; we are to walk

on the delectable mountains all the way.   Mark
you, we never can insist enough on the true joy of
the religious life.   We never can forget that to the
heavy-laden, Christ said, and says for ever, 'My
yoke is easy.'   But that is so interpreted sometimes, and the harder and sterner sayings are
so evaded, that religion seems to walk in silver
slippers.

But when I turn to another class of teachers—
and some of the greatest of every age are in it—
what impresses me is not the ease of things, but
the depth and difficulty of religion.   The gate
is narrow ; the way is strait and mountainous ;
the cross is heavy, and the flesh cries out against
it.   Let every student read Dr. Newman's
sermons if he would see that view of the religious
life expressed in matchless English.   That, then,
is the seeming contradiction.   These are the
two opposite conceptions.   The one says, 'If I
come to Jesus, happy shall I be.'   The other
says, 'If I find Him, if I follow, what His
guerdon here?   Many a sorrow, many a labour,
many a tear.'

Well, in our text there can be little question
that our Lord leans to the latter of these views.

It is a great thing to be an earnest Christian, it is a high calling to be a knight of that round table; let a man, says Jesus, deliberately sit down and count the cost, lest the fair fame of it be smirched and sullied by him. Nothing impresses us more in Jesus Christ than His insistence on quality, not quantity. He never hesitated to set the standard high, even though men should be offended at Him. It is better to be served by twenty loyal hearts, than by half a hundred undisciplined adventurers. Think it all out, says Christ. Sit down, count up the cost, find what it comes to. Rash promising is certain to make shipwreck. I want you to be still, and know that I am God.

Now I think it immensely increases our reverence for Jesus to find Him dealing thus with human souls. He never veils the hardship of His calling, He is so absolutely certain of its glory. When Drake and the gallant captains of Queen Elizabeth's time went out into the streets of Plymouth to get sailors, they told them quite frankly of the storms of the Pacific, and of the reefs in it, and of the fevers of Panama. They honoured their brave Devonshire comrades far

too much to get them to sign on under any false
pretences. But then there was the Spanish gold
and treasure, and the glory of it, and all England
to ring with it. And the men counted the cost
and signed for that daring service, in the spacious
times of great Elizabeth. And I honour our
Captain for dealing with men like that—the
press-gang is an un-Christlike instrument. Christ
says : You are a free man ; count the cost.
Life is before you : choose whom you will
serve. I offer you a cross, also a crown. I
offer you struggle, but there shall be victory.
You shall be lonely, yet lo, I am with you
always. You shall be restless, yet I will give
you rest. Was there ever a leader so frank,
so open, so brave, as the Master who is claiming you to-night ?

And it is just here that the service of our
Lord stands at opposite poles from the service
of sin. For the one thing that sin can never do
is to say to a man, 'Sit down and count the cost
of it.' Do you think that to-night's drunkard
ever counted the cost when men called him such
splendid company twenty years ago ? Do you
think that the man who has tried for, and missed,

life's prizes counted the cost when he was sowing his wild oats? Sin is too subtle, too sweet, too masterfully urgent, to give a man time for that arithmetic. 'Evil is wrought by want of thought, as well as want of heart.' If that young student who has come up for the Winter Session, and who has dropped in here, will only deliberately count the cost this evening ; if he will only remember he is in the grip of law that no repentance ever can annul; if he will think that as he sows this winter, so every coming winter will he reap, I think he will shake himself and say, 'Get thee behind me, Satan.' It is true that you cannot put old heads upon young shoulders. But don't we begin counting when we are little children? And half the battle of a man's life is won when he sits down and counts the cost. Sin will keep a man from that, by hook or crook. But 'come and let us reason together,' saith the Lord.

Of course we must distinguish this wise deliberation from a merely calculating and cowardly prudence. It is often the man who has counted the cost most earnestly, who shows a kind of splendid imprudence to the world. I mean that

what the world calls prudence is very often a
somewhat shallow thing. It does not run its
roots into the deeps ; it is really a kindlier name
for selfishness. And the man who has dwelt
alone with the great things, and who has been
touched by the hand of the Eternal, is not likely
in that sense to be worldly wise. I dare say
that everybody thought John Knox imprudent
when he insisted on preaching in St. Andrews,
though the Archbishop had warned him he
would slay him. I dare say everybody thought
Martin Luther imprudent, when he said he
would go to the Diet though every tile on the
housetops were a devil. But Knox and Luther
had been alone with God ; it was deliberate
action, and not reckless folly. They had counted
the cost for Scotland and for Christendom.

The fact is, that in all the highest courage
there is the element of quiet calculation. The
truest heroism always counts the cost. The
bravery of passion is not a shining virtue.
I think that a very ordinary man could storm
a rampart, if he were a soldier. They tell us
there is a wild forgetfulness of self in that last
rush that would fire the blood and thrill the

most timid. The test of courage is the long night
march, under the fire of invisible guns ; it is
the sentry duty in the darkness, when the
shadows and silence might shatter the strongest
nerve : I think that the man who deliberately
faces that, who goes through it quietly because
it is his duty, is just as worthy of the Victoria
Cross as the man who has won it in some more
splendid moment. No man, said one of Oliver
Cromwell, no man was a better judge than
Oliver of what might be achieved by daring.
Yet the true heroism of that noble soul was not
the heroism of the rash adventurer. He never
let texts do duty for tactics, says Mr. Morley.
I always admired the answer of that man who
was going forward with a comrade to some
dangerous duty. And his comrade looked at
him, and saw that his cheek was blanched. And
he laughed and said, 'I believe you are afraid.'
And the other, looking straight forward, said,
'Yes, I *am* afraid, and if you were half as afraid
as I am, you would go home.' Do not forget,
then, that when Jesus says, 'Count the cost,' He
is really sounding the note of the heroic. He
does not want any one on false pretences

He will not issue any lying prospectus. He comes to you and says, You are a thinking man, with powers that it will take eternity to ripen. Look life in the face. Look death in the. face. Sum it all up, measure the value of things. And if you do that quietly and earnestly, with sincere prayer to God to enlighten you, My claims, Christ means, shall so tower above all others, that I shall have your heart and your service from that hour.

I have been struck, too, in studying the Scriptures, to note how the great men there learned to count the cost. They were not suddenly dragged into the service. There was no unthinking and unreasoning excitement. God gave to every one of them a time of silence before their high endeavour. It was as if He laid His hand upon them and said, 'My child, go apart for a little, and count the cost.' Moses was forty days alone with God. Elijah was in the wilderness alone. Paul, touched by the finger of the Lord whom he had persecuted, took counsel of no flesh, but departed into the loneliness of Arabia. Moses, Elijah, Paul—yes, even Simon Peter going out into the night—were learning the deep lesson of our parable. And whenever I read of the temptations of Jesus, and of how the Spirit of God drove Him apart, and how Satan came and showed Him all the kingdoms, and taught Him a less costly way to sovereignty than by the sweat of Gethsemane and the water and blood of Calvary—whenever I read that and recall how He stood fast, I feel that our Saviour had counted the cost Himself. We shall never understand the calm persistence of the glorious company of martyrs and of saints till we go back to that quiet hour at the beginning when they faced every difficulty, weighed every cross, forecast the future, looked at life whole, and then, having counted the cost like reasonable men, took up their stand upon the side of God. A blind acceptance may be justifiable sometimes. But the great hearts were never led that way.

Now I want you to join that reasonable company. I do not know that that is popular doctrine, but I want to get the young men back to the Church of Christ again, and I am willing to risk unpopularity for that. 'Come, let us reason together,' saith the Lord. 'Sit down and

count the cost,' says Jesus Christ.   I do not ask
any man to become a Christian blindly.   It is
the most reasonable act in the whole world.   For
the sake of a saved life and of a rich eternity
you ought to make that reckoning immediately.

THE SENDING OF THE SWORD

I came not to send peace, but a sword.—Matt. x. 34.

THERE seems to be a glaring contradiction between this word and some other words of Jesus. Some of the most familiar gospel-words —words that shine down like stars on the world's darkness—speak of Jesus as the great peace-bringer. 'Peace I leave with you. My peace I give unto you. Not as the world giveth give I unto you.' Yet here, 'I came not to send peace, but a sword.' The point I wish you to observe in passing is Christ's disregard for superficial consistency. Life proves many a proposition to be true that logic would readily demonstrate as false. And the strange thing about the words of Christ is, that while they seem to contradict each other at the bar of reason, they link themselves together into perfect harmony when we go forward in the strength of them. Are you fond of arguing about Christ's teachings? You may argue till doomsday and never find their power. They are words of life; meant to be lived out; there is no argument in all the armoury like action. And it is only as we set our faces heavenward, making these statutes our song in the house of our pilgrimage : only as we view every new morning as a new opportunity of putting Christ to proof; it is only thus, through the gathering experience of days, that we awaken to their power and truth. I notice in the engines of our river-steamers that there are rods that move backward as well as rods that move forward. A child would say they were fighting with each other, and that half of the engines were going the wrong way. But though half the engines seem to go the wrong way, there is no question that the ship is going the right way : out of the smoke and stir of the great city into the bays where the peace of God is resting. So with the words of Christ that seem to oppose each other. Make them the driving power of the soul : and the oppositions will not hinder progress, and the contradictions will reveal their unity, and you shall be brought to your desired haven.

So to our text; and there are two lights in

which I wish to set it. (1) The coming of Christ sends a sword into the heart. (2) The coming of Christ sends a sword into the home.

First, then : The coming of Christ sends a sword into the heart.

Now this is exactly what I should have expected when I remembered the penalties of gain. For everything a man achieves there is a price to pay. There comes a wound with everything we win. Think of the knowledge of nature that we now possess, thanks to the genius and toil of Darwin. It has thrown a flood of light upon the world and brought us nearer to the ways of God. Yet it has shown us the struggle for existence, raging with a ferocity our fathers never dreamed of ; it has revealed to us nature red in tooth and claw ; it has given us ears for the sound of deadly battle back of the glory of the summer's evening, so that for many of us the world can never seem so fair again, nor the song of birds so innocently sweet. All knowledge, whatever joy it brings with it, brings with it in the other hand a sword. All love, though it kindles the world into undreamed-of brightness, has a note in its music of unrest and agony. Every advance mankind has ever made, every new gift or endowment man has won, holds in its grasp new possibilities of pain.

It is through thoughts like these that I come to understand how the coming of Christ into the heart must send a sword there. To receive Christ is to receive the Truth ; it is to have the Spirit of Love breathing within us : and if truth and love always bring sorrow with them, I shall expect the coming of Christ to be with pain. I have no doubt there are some here to-night to whom Christ came, and made them very happy. You will never forget the hour of your conversion, when, as by the rending of a veil, the night was gone, and the trees in the forest clapped their hands before you, and every star in the heavens shone more brightly. A true experience; a very real experience : there are those here who look back on such an hour. But Jesus does not always come that way. He comes with the sword as well as with the song. He comes to banish the old shallow happiness ; to break the ice that was over the deep waters ; to touch the chords that had never given their music ; to open the eyes to the hills above the cloud. And if He has come to you thus, so that you are not happier but consumed with a passion of divine discontent, I bid you in God's name go forward—it is Christ with the sword, but it is still the Christ. It is a great thing to feel like singing. Perhaps it is greater still to feel like struggling. This one thing I do, forgetting the things that are behind, I press towards the mark.

There are three ways in which the coming of Christ into the heart sends a sword there. I can only briefly touch on these three ways to-night. Christ opens up the depths of sin within us; that is one. We see what we are in the light of His perfection. We were tolerably contented with our character once, but when Christ comes we are never that again. Like the sheep that look clean enough among the summer grass, but against the background of the virgin snow look foul; so you and I never know how vile we are until the background of our life is Christ. You would have thought that when Christ filled Peter's net, Peter would have been ecstatically happy; but instead of that you have Simon Peter crying, 'Depart from me, O Lord, I am a sinful man.' Christ came to Simon Peter with the sword;

showed him himself; taught him how dark he was. And whenever the sword-stroke of an indwelling Saviour cuts into the deeps of a man's heart, the wound is very likely to be sore.

And then Christ calls us to a lifelong warfare. The note of warfare rings through the whole New Testament. The spirit is quickened now to crave for spiritual things, and the flesh and the spirit must battle till the grave. I knew a student who had been to Keswick and had drunk deep of the teaching of that school. And very noble teaching it is when nobly grasped. And he came back to Scotland in a kind of rapture; everything was to be easy evermore. And he went to one of our most saintly and notable ministers to tell him about this new-found way to holiness, and the minister (with his beautiful smile) looked at him and said, ' Ah, sir, it will be a sore *warstle* till the end.' For we wrestle not against flesh and blood, but against principalities and powers and spiritual darkness. And the evil that I would not, that I do, and the good I would that do I not. Paul knew the peace of God that passed all understanding, yet to Paul the Saviour came bearing the sword.

But above all, it is by heightening our ideal that the old peace goes and the pain begins. It is in the new conception of what life may be that the sword-stroke cuts into the heart. We are no more the children of time and space. We are the children of glorious immortality. We are launching out on to a career that will advance and deepen for ever and for ever. And do you think that the birth of a mighty thought like that can be accomplished without wound or pain? Whenever the horizon widens there is sorrow. The sword of Christ smites through the thongs that bind us. The sword of Christ cuts down the veil that shadows us. The sword of Christ makes free play for our manhood; we step into our liberty through Him. And if, with all that, there comes a haunting pain and an unrest that may become an agony, remember that Christ came to send the sword.

But I pass on now: so, secondly and lastly, Christ comes to send a sword into the home.

Did you ever think how true that was of Nazareth? Did you ever reflect on our text in the light of that home? There was not a cottager in all the village but would think of one home they knew when they heard this. Joseph and Mary—was there any home in Nazareth on which the sunshine of heaven seemed to rest so sweetly? The peace of mutual love and trust lay on it, like a benediction from the green hills that sheltered it. Then into that quiet home came Jesus Christ, and the point of the sword has touched the heart of Joseph. And he was minded to put Mary away quietly, for the great love he had to her. Then came the flight to Egypt; then Jesus in the Temple—ah, yes! the sword is going deeper now. And when the public ministry began, and He was put to scorn, rejected, crucified, I think the sword had smitten that quiet home. It might have been so peaceful and so happy, with the laughter of children and the joy of motherhood. It might have been so peaceful and so happy if God had never honoured it like this. But Jesus was born there, and that made all the difference. It could never be the quiet home again. Gethsemane was coming, Calvary was coming; a sword was going to pierce through Mary's heart. He came not to send peace, but a sword.

Now I think that still in many and many a

home the coming of Jesus spells out unrest like
that. When a young man or woman in a
worldly home takes a definite stand, comes out
and out for Christ, then the father and mother
and every brother and sister will understand the
meaning of this text. There is no outward
quarrelling—how could there be when all the
family are members of the Church ? But the
new enthusiasm and the new consecration and the
new wholeheartedness for Jesus Christ—all well
enough at the distance of the pulpit, but now
brought into the bosom of the family—cause unrest,
uneasiness, and irritation there, and that is Christ
coming with the sword. I quite admit the sword
is needlessly sharpened sometimes by the pride
and arrogance of the young convert. I have had
cases in my ministry where all my sympathy went
out to the unconverted brothers. But this I
want to say. Is there any young man or woman
here whose difficulty in deciding for Christ is the
life at home ? Well, then, be very humble ; do
not obtrude yourself ; remember your ignorance,
remember your youth ; but as you have a life to
live, and as you have a death to die, and as you
have a God to meet before the Throne, do not let

father or mother or the happiest home that ever
cradled man keep you from closing with the call
of God. If there must be trouble, then trouble
there must be. To thine own self be true.
As man to man Christ says to you to-night,
'I come not to send peace, but a sword.'

A word to the children of sorrow as I close.
A word to the fathers and to the mothers here.
I want you to remember there is another way in
which Christ has brought the sword into the
home. For home itself has a wealth of meaning
in it, that it never would have had save for the
Gospel. And the natural love of the mother for
her child has been deepened and glorified since
Jesus came. Brotherhood, sisterhood, fatherhood, motherhood, childhood, you do not know
how little these words meant once. And if *now*
they speak to us of what is truest and tenderest,
of ties unsurpassably delicate and strong, it is the
love of Christ, it is the revelation of the Father,
it is the touch of our Brother that has achieved the
change. And what is the other side of that rich
heritage? Ask any Christian mother for the
answer. Find out if her heart never bleeds over
her child ; if she has not hours of haunting and

torturing fears. Develop love, and you develop sorrow. Deepen the heart-life, and you deepen suffering. It is by doing that, through all the centuries, that Christ has brought the sword into our homes. The Stoic said, 'Dry up these fountains of feeling'; so he made a solitude and called it peace. But Christ deepened and cleansed life's well-springs here, and that very deepening has brought the sword. I think it is worth it. I would not be a Stoic. It is better to live vividly, spite of the pain, than to have the finger-tips of all the angels grope at a heart of steel. After all, if He smiteth, He will bind up again. If He woundeth, yet He will make us whole. The sword, like Excalibur swung by the arm of Bedivere, shall flash and sink into the deeps for ever, when we wake in the eternal morning of the Lord.

WASTED GAINS

The slothful man roasteth not that which he took in hunting.—
Prov. xii. 27.

A PROVERB is wisdom crystallised. It is the effort to sum up in a few homely words what all feel to be true. Men like to hear their own thoughts in pithy speech, and that is what a true proverb achieves. That is the secret of its hold, at certain stages of a people's life. A proverb is not philosophy, nor is it poetry ; yet both philosophy and poetry meet in the proverb. It takes a philosophic view, then clothes it in poetic speech ; it does not want to preach, it wants to picture. There is a stage in every life when we almost need to have our wisdom so. And in the life of peoples comes a period when proverbs rule like autocrats, only more wisely.

Our text then is a proverb, a compressed parable. First let us see the picture in it

The slothful man roasteth not what he took in hunting. It is the picture of a hunter—he is a sportsman, but a lazy fellow. But some fine autumn morning this hunter wakens early. The air is keen ; the dogs are baying ; the old enthusiasm of the chase stirs in his heart. He will go forth and hunt to-day, and his right hand has not lost its cunning. So far all is well. Laden with bird and beast he gets back to his tent. Then comes the waste, the sin. The impulse is gone ; the morning's glow is dead—he cannot be troubled cooking what he caught. So bird and beast lie there, day after day ; until for very shame the hunter casts them out. Unused, they become useless. It is a case of wasted gains. For all the good he gets from them, he might as well have stayed at home, and left his bow hanging upon the wall.

Such is the picture. Now do you see the meaning of it ? It may be, that huntsman is not far away. By toil, by tears, by sharing in the toil and tears of others, our life is rich in gains. Trophies have fallen to our bow, and to the bow of the nation with which we are one, and to the bow of the gospel we believe ; and we have never roasted what we took in hunting. The gains are wasted ; the trophies are unused.

I want to run that thought out into various spheres of life ; and first, the wasted gains in bodily life. Take speech or sight. We talk sometimes of speech and sight as gifts. And in a deep sense they are gifts—gifts of God. But for His touch, so exquisitely skilful, these powers could never link us in such mystic harmony to the great world without. But do not forget that if speech and sight are gifts, they are also gains. It took the exercise of weeks in infancy before that eye of yours distinguished this from that. It took the lispings and babblings of months before your tongue fashioned a single word. And for years more there dawned never a day but you were practising the mystery of speech. And now? Compare the possibilities of sight with what you see. Contrast the possibilities of speech with what you say ; and are not speech and sight terribly wasted gains ? Was it worth while toiling through childish years only to see and say what you saw and said to-day ? I think we shall all be ready to confess that we have not roasted what we took in hunting.

Again, there are wasted gains in our social life. Take friendship, for example. Think for a moment of the toil it cost to make a single friend. Have you forgotten the first approaches, the long misunderstanding, the failures and the tears, the gradual dawn? Don't you recall how painfully you won your way into that other life, fighting each step under the banner of friendship, gaining this rampart and now that, until you stood alone, victorious, within the secret room? It was a gain, that friendship; won after toil as strenuous as any hunter's. It was a spoil, a trophy, of the like of which life has but few. And it was yours to use and to enjoy, till God should separate the twain by death.

Ah wasted gains! That friendship, built like some cathedral, to-night is lying in ruins. New interests have so thronged into your life, and business has so engrossed you in these eager days, that you have had no time, nor any heart, this many a day, to keep your friendships in repair. Think of your home, sir! Think of your wife! Life was once full of these little kindnesses that are far more to some hearts than gold or silver. Where are they now? Have you no time now

from your business and your paper and your golf
for your wife at all ? These wasted gains are the
tragedy of home. Not sorrow and not poverty
and not the white coffin of your little child—that
is no tragedy. God may bless that to bring the
sunshine back, and link the separating hearts
again. The tragedy is the passing of love's
kindness ; the sloth that lets us squander what
we won ; the waste of the sweet gains of golden
days.

Once more, there are wasted gains in our public
and our national life. It is a commonplace to say
that all our privileges and rights as citizens have
been dearly bought. But after all, half of our
life is spent in finding out that commonplaces
are true, so let us hear this commonplace again.
Our privileges were bought for us at a great price.
Our humblest liberties were won in battle. The
charters of our rights are written in blood. Men
have been labouring, battling, dying since ever
Britain was a nation, to give us whatsoever of
liberty we enjoy. Read over your history again
—what is it all ? Is it the record of the corona-
tion of the kings and of the deaths of queens?
It is the story of man's spirit, hampered, op-

pressed, confined, yet always struggling for its own. It is the record of the soul, crying and not to be denied, for its God-given rights. That is what history means, if it means anything. It is the tale of how our gains were won. And every one of them, I shall make no exception, is marked with struggle and is wet with tears. And oh, the pity of it, how we waste them !

There is our restful Sunday, and it was dearly bought. But every country road and country inn on Sunday is thronged with men who never think of God. There is the open Bible, and it was dearly bought, yet now it is every book before the Bible. There is our liberty of worship, and it was dearly bought, yet, come a rainy Sunday, and half the churches in the city are unfilled.

And there is our right of voting too, of moulding public life and sharing in it, and that was dearly bought. And hundreds of men and women are so careless that they will sit at home, or visit, or go to work, and never trouble to record their vote. We understand all ages but our own. We grapple with all problems but the problems at our doors. We hear all cries except the cries that rise to-day from a great

city's need. It is not right. We are not roasting
what we took in hunting.

Lastly, in our moral and spiritual life there is
the same tale of wasted gains. Had we but used
all we have learned ; had we but held by all that
suffering taught us ; had we but clung to what
we wrestled for, we should be nearer heaven to-
night. But we have squandered it like any
prodigal, and flung it to the winds, and almost
all the lessons are to learn again !

Here is a man who had a serious illness once.
It brought him to the gates of death. And lying
there things looked very different from what they
had looked before. He caught some glimpses of
God then, and of the infinite worth of eternal
things, and of the value of the soul. It was a
gain inestimable. And now to-night that man is
better. That man is here—in church. And what
of God ? Forgotten. What of eternal things ?
Forgotten. What of the soul ? Forgotten. The
tides of the world's life have swept them out.
It is a wasted gain.

Here is a father who lost his child once. And
in that first great woe he knelt, and broken-
hearted asked for pardon for his sin, and vowed

his life to God till the day brake.   And he is here,
that father—with lips as careless, and with life
as worldly, as though the child he loved had
never died.

Here is a young fellow who set himself once to
master his besetting sin.   And he did master it,
thanks be to God.   He cast it out, and trod it
under foot, and walked with a new light upon
his face—and we all saw it.   That was five years
ago, five months ago.   And now, slowly and
silently in the unguarded moments, the serpent
has been creeping back to its place again.   The
gain of that great effort has been wasted, and
the old habit is the master still !

Brethren and sisters !   I charge you to remember this.   Squander your gains, and God will
take them from you.   Neglect your talents, and
God will take your talents back.   Misuse your
sight, and God will rob you of the power to see.
Despise your teachings, and God will not teach
you any more.

Only not yet !   not yet !   God is still gracious !
Man of one talent, of one gain, God has not
reached His hand out yet, and taken that gain
away.   Out of all waste and failure thou mayst

yet organise victory. 'I can do all things through
Christ who strengtheneth me.' What, Paul!
couldst *thou* do that, a man of like passions with
ourselves? Then so may we. We can still use,
thanks to the grace that saves us, the spoils that
were dearly taken in the hunting.

UNDETECTED LOSSES

Grey hairs are here and there upon him, yet he knoweth not.—
Hos. vii. 9.

OUR text refers to the northern kingdom of
Israel whose decay was so keenly felt by Hosea.
That kingdom—the kingdom of the tribes—had
started well. It was a protest on behalf of
liberty. It had the benediction of prophets at
its birth, it had Elijah and Elisha to inspire it.
Cradled in the fairest part of Palestine, enjoying
a freedom to which Judah was a stranger, the
possibilities of such a state seemed boundless ;
yet when Hosea wrote, the dream was dying ;
the possibilities had passed away. Israel had lost
the energy of youth. The quick eye and the
strong hand were gone. Israel was falling into
sad descrepitude. There was a touch of moral
senility in Israel. And the worst of it was that
Israel did not know it, she was unconscious of
the tremendous drop. The nation had suffered

the worst of all national losses, and the losses were undetected losses. Grey hairs were here and there upon him, yet he knew it not.

Our text, then, leads us very naturally to the general thought of undetected losses. And it is on that subject—the things we lose without knowing we are losing them—that I wish to speak a little to-night. Some losses reveal themselves at once. There are things which, lost, leave the heart blank and desolate. We see at a glance, by the naked gap among the grass, that some tree has been uprooted there; but many of life's worst losses are not so. There is loss, but there is no sense of loss. Virtues, ideals, things bright and strong and beautiful, steal away silently from us in the dark. They used to say, 'The gods have feet of wool'—and what is divine departs on feet of wool. If we could only *see* our own deterioration, perhaps we would cry to God about it more. But our best goes without any sound of trumpet, and we never dream how poor we have become. 'Grey hairs are here and there upon us, and we know it not.'

Of course I know that the other side is true.

If some of our worst losses are unnoticed, some
of our gains are undetected also. The fact is
that all that makes life rich has a way of coming,
as of going, silently. The kingdom of Christ
is the very highest manhood, and the kingdom
cometh not with observation. It is very perilous
to be sure we are growing good. Moses wist
not that his face shone. I think that no one
would have been more surprised than David had
he been told he was the man after God's own
heart. Life is not all a battle or a race ; life
is a walk with God, life is a growth. And as in
walking with some pure-souled friend we are won
towards purity and do not know it, and as in all
growth from the seed to summer beauty, there
is, as it were, an undetected movement, so in the
truest life there is a sweet unconsciousness—except
ye become as little children. Like Milton, we are
blind to our own poem. Like Beethoven, we are
deaf to our own music. We reach the highest,
and we lose the highest, and we know it not.

I think our Lord was voicing that deep truth
when He said, ' If the salt have lost its savour.'
All loss of character, loss of a fair name, all loss
of influence, ideal, spirituality, is typified in the

salt that has lost its savour. The salt was white yesterday : is it less white to-day? And it weighed five ounces when you measured it last week. Will it weigh one scruple less to-morrow ? Look at it, handle it, take it externally, and measure it : it has not changed or altered in the least, has it? Yet yesterday it was fit for the food of man, and to-day it is only fit to be trodden under foot. Something has gone from it that no balance can measure. Something impalpable, invisible, imponderable. You might have watched all night into the morning, and you would never have seen the savour go. And our Lord means that as the salt loses its savour, so you and I lose what is best and brightest. The best and the brightest never says good-bye. It does not touch us on the brow when we are sleeping, and tell us the ship is ready : it must go. Under the pressure of a worldly city, and by the gradual slackening of a man's grasp of God, through minute failures and infinitesimal cowardices, by yieldings that are almost imperceptible, it is thus that the ideal dies away, it is thus that influence, power, womanhood are lost. I wonder if that is going

on to-night, here?   'Grey hairs are here and
there upon him, and he knows not.'

Now, can we explain these undetected losses?
Is it possible to discover why we are thus blind?
Well, I think that often our losses go unnoticed
because of the stir and excitement of our life.
Just as the soldier in the rush of battle, when the
bugle has sounded and the bayonet is fixed—just
as that soldier, charging with a cheer, is struck,
and hardly feels that he is wounded ; so it may
be that in the busy city, where many a man is
fighting just as keenly as they ever fought at
Alma or at Inkerman, it may be that there too
men hardly feel that the life-blood has begun
to ebb away.   We very readily forget ourselves
when we are privileged to listen to exquisite
music ; and when the music of life and of the
world is sweet, it is easy to forget the still small
voice.   Do you think that the prodigal felt his
loss of home so long as his money lasted in the
far country?   His new-found liberty was far too
sweet for that—the dicing and the dancing and
the wine.   I mean that when life is crowded and
tumultuous, whether it be with business or with
pleasure, a man may lose much and never feel

the loss. Hence one of the great ministries of sickness. It says to us, 'Come ye apart and rest a while.' We recognise ourselves in the dark hours of suffering, when the drearier night succeeds the dreary day. It is only then the truth breaks in on us. We see what we have been, what we have lost. Alone with his conscience and alone with God, a man's losses are not unnoticed any more.

I think, too, that a reason for our blindness lies in this, that with all loss there comes some kind of gain. There is no such thing as dead loss in the universe. We live in a universe of compensation. Spring goes, but the glory of Summer comes. Summer departs, but the wealth of Autumn is left. We should be blind to half the glories of the forest if the gale did not sweep its million leaves away. Poor Lot, when he made his foolish choice, lost Abraham's company ; but he gained Sodom, and Sodom was choicely situated. And the prodigal gained liberty and pleasure, and the gain made him oblivious of his home. Ah, brother, if all that was best and highest passed from our life and left a dead blank behind it, then in that very moment we should feel the loss, and crave to have the highest back again. But life is far more intricate than that, thanks to its principle of loss and gain. You lose an Abraham, and gain a Sodom. You lose the saintly purity of wifehood, and gain the stolen waters that are sweet. You lose a father, but you gain your liberty. You lose a conscience, but you gain a fortune. And the point I want to impress on you is this, that often these lower gains are so alluring, so sweet, so satisfying to every sense, that we never see how the best is dying out of us. 'Grey hairs are on us, and we know it not.'

But the great cause of our neglected losses lies in the gradual and slow method of the loss. There are men whose hair has whitened in a night. I warrant you they saw that in the morning. But it is not of that Hosea speaks, when he uses the happy figure of our text. All that was best had perished out of Israel. Why was Israel ignorant of that ? The loss had come so slowly, surely, silently, Israel had failed to detect it when it came. If all the birds ceased singing in the summer, the dullest city ear would note the silence. If the forest were swept bare

by one swift gale, the blindest of us would find
cause for wonder. But the music of the woods
ceases so gradually, and the trees are stripped
so silently and slowly, that winter is with us,
songless and desolate, before we have eyes for
what is being lost. Some sins carry immediate
penalties ; their consequences leap into light at
once. The moment a man commits them he
is ruined. And we know that : perhaps therefore we avoid them. But there is another ruin
quite as sure as that, wrought silently through
deterioration of the years, and it steals on the
spirit of a man so gradually that grey hairs are
on him and he knows it not. In one of the
most charming of Charles Dickens's stories, the
heroine—Esther Summerson—had a fever. And
when she rose from the bed of fever the sweet,
pure beauty of her face was gone. She saw it at
once. It was too evident to miss. She had to
accept it as a cross from God. But there are
other ways in which beauty disappears. Ten
years of worldliness, and utter thoughtlessness,
and frivolous selfishness, and an unkindly heart—
all that will do it quite as well as fever. And yet
the woman hardly understands why no one ever

calls her beautiful now. I tell you that is a parable of character. It is the silent dying away of what is best that is the great tragedy in this great city. Lightning is dangerous. So is dry rot, remember. 'Grey hairs are here and there upon him, and he knows not.'

Now just remember—and with this I close— that sooner or later all losses will be known. How you are living, whether or not you pray, the secret carelessness, the buried sin—the day is coming, far sooner than you think, when that shall not be a secret any more. Sudden temptation comes, or change of circumstances ; a call, or a crisis perhaps, or if not these, eternity ; and all that we have made of common days, and all the sappings of principle we shrouded, will be written out so that he that runs may read. Samson arose and shook himself as at other times, and he wist not that his strength was gone from him : but 'the Philistines are upon thee, Samson,' and he learned his undetected losses then. Be not deceived ; God is not mocked ; whatsoever a man soweth, that shall he also reap.

WHEN THE CHILD-SPIRIT DIES

Of such is the kingdom of heaven.—Matt. xix. 14.

It is a beautiful thought, of such are the kingdom
of heaven. It is a beautiful conception, daring
and fresh as it is beautiful, that the one attribute
of all the citizens of God must be the possession
of the childlike heart. We need not be learned,
though it is sweet to be learned ; we need not
be gifted, though God be thanked for gifts. But
we must be childlike ; that is the one necessity.
Christ takes an unalterable stand on that.

Now of course to be childlike is one thing ;
and it is quite another to be childish. I sometimes fear we have so confused the two, that a
certain contempt has touched the nobler of them
—we use our common words so carelessly, and
treat that magnificent instrument of speech so
lightly. To be childlike is to have the spirit of
the child, to have the touch of the divine about
us still. It is to live freshly in a glad fresh

world, with a thousand avenues into the everywhere out of this dull spot that we call *now*.
But to be childish is to be immature ; to have no
grip of things, never to face facts squarely ; and
he is a poor Christian who lives so. In understanding, says the apostle, I would have you men.
It is one distinguishing glory of our Lord that
He looked the worst in the face, and called it
bad. But the guileless heart, and the soul that
can serve and sing, because there is love and home
and fatherland about it—all that is childlike—
like the children—and of such is the kingdom of
heaven.

There can be little doubt, too, that in claiming
the child-spirit Jesus was reaching up to the very
highest in man. ' Wisdom,' says Wordsworth in
his own quiet way—so helpful in these noisy days
—' Wisdom is ofttimes nearer when we stoop,
than when we soar,' and Jesus, stooping to the
little children, was really rising to the crown of
life. Show me the greatest men in human history
—the men who were morally and nobly great—
and I shall show you in every one of them tokens
and traces of the childlike heart. It is the
middle-men, the worldly middle-men, the men of

one talent who bury it in the napkin, it is *these*
who are locked into their prison-house, and have
lost the happy daring of the child.   Great souls,
with the ten talents flaming into genius, live in a
world that is so full of God, that men say they
are imprudent, careless ; and Jesus sees that they
are little children.   Who was it that defined a
genius as a man who keeps unsullied through
the stern teaching of the years the spirit of the
child ?   I think that Christ would have liked that
definition.   There is genius in childhood ; there
is childhood in genius too.   ' He hath put down
the mighty from their seats, and exalted them
of low degree.'

And you cannot read the story of Jesus Christ
without feeling that to the very close of it the
child-spirit was alive in Him.   ' A little child
shall lead them,' said the prophet ; do you think
it was only a poetic fancy ?   The Bible is too
terribly in earnest to have any margin for poetic
fancies.   When I study the records of the life of
Jesus, and stumble on some unfathomable mystery,
immediately I find my heart responding, ' This is
the Son of God.'   And when I find Him healing
the Syrophenician's daughter, raising the widow's

son, or weeping in infinite pity by the grave—' This is the Son of Man.'   But when I light on these passages about the lilies ; about the sparrow falling, and the raven who toiled not ; then, in a thousand touches such as these, fresh, penetrating, wonderful, I feel that after all the prophet was right—a little child shall lead them.   No scoffing hardened Him.   No disappointment soured Him. No pain dulled the keen edge of His love.   He still believed, spite of Iscariot.   He had still a Father, spite of Calvary.   And that sweet spirit, as of a little child, has been the dew of heaven to the world.

The spirit of the child, then, never died in Jesus.   I wonder if it has died in you ?   It dies away so slowly and so gradually, under the pressure of a worldly city, that we hardly notice how far we have drifted.   But the greatest losses are the losses we never observe ; the crumblings in secret till this or that is ruined ; the stealing away of the dearest in the dark ; and there is no loss more tragic for a soul than the loss of that spirit of the child.

You ask me why ?   I think there are three reasons ; there are three penalties that follow when the child-spirit dies, and the first is, that we cease to be receptive. The joy of childhood is its receptivity. The greatest duty of it is to receive. The child knows nothing of a haunting past yet, and it is not yet anxious about the future. Its time is *now*, with its magnificent content, and now is God's time too, do not forget. But you and I have so overlaid this present with yesterday's sin and with to-morrow's project, that we have little heart for the message that comes to-day. We are not receptive as the little child is, we do not welcome impressions and angels now. And so we grow very commonplace and dull; there is plenty of dust about us, and no dew. O brother, let the dead past bury its dead! Do not be living in a quenched yesterday. And take no anxious thought about to-morrow. Consider the lilies; be a child again. To feel the eternal in this passing moment, to catch the rustle of God's garment now, not to be burdened with a vain regret, not to be peering forward through the curtain; all that, with the open eye and feeling heart, is to be childlike. And of such is the kingdom of heaven.

No doubt it is that very receptivity that makes

the little children dwell apart. I have long thought that the aloofness of the Christian, his isolation in the busiest life, was closely akin to the aloofness of the child. You talk of loneliness ?—I tell you there are few such lonely creatures as little children. And they are lonely, not because of sorrow ; and not, thank God, because their lives are empty. They dwell apart, because they live in their own world, bright, wonderful, with its own visions and voices, and you and I never touch even with our finger-tips these ivory gates and golden. What I suggest is that the isolation of the saint is like the isolation of the child. For the Christian also dwells apart, but not in the solitude of emptiness. He has *his* world, just as the children have ; old things have passed away from him in Christ. And in that new creation where the Saviour reigns, and which the worldly heart has never seen, there is a peopled isolation like that of the little children, for of such is the kingdom of heaven.

Once more, when the child-spirit dies, then the simplicity of faith is gone. There is an exquisite purity about the faith of children ; sometimes they make us blush—they trust us so. Intensely eager, inquisitively curious; why? why? from the sunrise, to the sunset—but all the time how they are trusting us! Ah, if we had only trusted God like that! It is something to be trusted, if only by a helpless babe, and even God is happier when we trust Him. But better than to be trusted, is to trust; to walk by faith and not by sight; and when the spirit of the child dies out, it is not possible to walk that way again. For when we cease to be childlike we grow worldly, and to be worldly is always to be faithless; and one great danger of this commercial city is to develop faithless worldly men. I have no doubt you call me an idle dreamer because I plead for the child-spirit in the city. But it is better to be a dreamer than a coward, and woe is me if I preach not the gospel. 'Of such is the kingdom of heaven'—minister! 'Of such is the kingdom of heaven'—merchant! 'Of such is the kingdom of heaven'—schoolmaster, doctor, workman, servant! Are you of such? It is not my question. I only pass it on from Jesus Christ!

Lastly, when the child-spirit dies, then the feeling of wonder disappears. For the child is

above all else a wonderer, and is set in the centre
of a wonderful world. There is nothing common
or unclean for children ; all things are big with
wonder for the bairn. The rolling of the wagon
in the street, and the gathering banks of cloud
down by the sunset ; and the opening flower, and
the father's morning kindness, and the mother's
stories, and the birthday joy—the little magicians
so trick them out with glory, that they make
the pomp of emperors ridiculous. Childhood, as
of one our poets sang, is—

> ' The hour
> Of glory in the grass, of splendour in the flower.'

What a poor thing is life when the wonder of
it all passes away ! I remember a magnificent
sermon by John Ker, that master in the great art
of spiritual preaching, and this is the title of it,
' God's word suited to man's sense of wonder.'
' I had rather,' said Ruskin, ' live in a cottage and
wonder at everything, than live in Warwick
Castle and wonder at nothing.' You have all
felt the *trials* of existence, I want you to feel the
wonder of it now ; and the great wonder that the
Lord should be your Shepherd, and should have

died upon Calvary for you. His name shall be called Wonderful—become a child again, and feel it so. For except ye be born again, ye cannot see the kingdom ; and of such is the kingdom of heaven.

THE LEISURE OF FAITH

He that believeth shall not make haste.—Is. xxviii. 16.

I THINK we shall all agree that in the life of our modern city there is recognisable the note of haste. One has only to watch one of our crowded streets to detect the pressure at the back of life. Life is more urgent than it used to be, the quietude of an older day is passing. The stream had still and shadowed reaches in it once, but to-day it hurries forward very swiftly.

Now it is notable that with that greater haste there is found, without any question, a lesser faith. There is a certain shrinking of the faculty of faith in the organism of our complex life. I am no pessimist, and I trust that none of you are. Life, for all its sorrow, is too real, too deep, too rich, to write that name of failure on its brow. But the most cheerful optimist cannot be blind to this, that faith, and reverence which is the child of faith, are not conspicuous in our modern city;

and the singular thing is, that with that decline of faith we should have witnessed the increase of hurry. Did you ever think that these features were connected? The Bible affirms it in the clearest manner. You say that the absence of restfulness in modern life springs from the fiercer struggle for existence. But the Bible goes a great deal deeper than that : the want of rest is rooted in want of trust. Depend upon it, he that believeth *not* is always in danger of feverish impatience. Depend upon it, that to the end of time, he that believeth shall not make haste.

Of course, it is very necessary for clear thinking to distinguish the haste of our text from strenuous speed. Every one who is at all in earnest about things feels the push and the pull to get his life-work done ; but a strenuous and resolute forwardness such as that is very different from the spirit of haste. 'Unhasting but unresting' should be the motto on every Christian's coat of arms. It is impossible that a true Christian should be a sluggard. Such new conceptions of life have dawned on him ; duty, and service, and the building up of character, are so expanded when God has touched the soul, that as

with the stirring music of the trumpet we are
called to redeem the time because the days are
evil.   But the man who hastes never redeems the
time.   You never redeem anything by hurrying
up.   And it is of that impatience, so closely akin to
fickleness—and an age of hurry is extraordinarily
fickle—it is of that impatience which knows no
inward quietude, and which robs life of its music
and its march, that the prophet is speaking
here.   He that believeth shall run and not be
weary.   He that believeth shall press toward the
mark.   He that believeth—God to his tardy feet
has promised to lend the swiftness of the roe.
But spite of that—nay, because of that—he that
believeth shall not make haste.

I like to apply our text to hasty judgments.
He that believeth shall not make haste to judge.
It is amazing how rashly and how recklessly we
pass severe judgments on each other.   There is
nothing harder than suspense of judgment in our
daily intercourse with men and women.   Even
the kindliest are in danger of prejudging, and
those who are not kindly do so constantly.   Now
do you see how we are to escape that sin ?   Do
you observe the secret of suspended judgment ?

It is not a matter of caution after all—he that
believeth shall not make haste to judge.   In all
disparagement there is a lack of faith.   In every
hasty summing up of character what is really
revealed is our own want of trust.   If we only
believed in our brother a little more, if we only
credited the divine within him ; if we only realised
that under the outward man there is a hidden man
of the heart striving and struggling, we should
be readier to think more kindly than we do.   I
want you to believe that under all disguise there
is a spark of the divine fire in every heart.   I
want you to believe that God is not far away even
from the life that you and I call godless.   He
that believeth in the love and patience of Heaven,
and in the image of God, defaced but not destroyed, will not make haste to judge.

Again, I think our text is full of meaning for
those who are in a great hurry to enjoy, and
perhaps the haste to be rich and taste life's
pleasures was never so markedly felt as it is now.
It is always a difficult thing to wait.   David was
never more saintly in his life than just when he
waited patiently for God.   But to-day, when the
means of enjoyment are so multiplied and the

music of the world is doubly sweet, the monotony of duty has become doubly irksome. It is very hard to be bound to that desk all day, while the golden hours of youth are flying so quickly. It is very hard from morning till weary night to be standing behind the counter in that warehouse, when life might be so rich and many-coloured if only there were a little liberty and leisure. Has not one of our own poets, himself a minister of the gospel, sung, ' Gather the rosebuds while ye may, old time is still aflying ' ? Hence springs a certain rebellion at our lot, a craving for immediate satisfaction ; a bitter willingness to forget the morrow if only we can snatch some pleasure now ; and to all men and women who are tempted so—and multitudes are tempted so to-day—comes the stern word of the eternal God, ' He that believeth shall not make haste.' The modern catechism asks ' What is man's chief end ?' and the answer it gives is ' Man's chief end is to enjoy *life*.' But the older catechism was wiser when it answered ' Man's chief end is to enjoy *God*,' and God can only be enjoyed, be sure of it, in the sphere of duty and along the line of work. Outside of that, the presence of God is

lost, and the cup is always bitter when that is lost.
Life has not been given us to enjoy, life has
been given us to use ; and I fancy you can use
it better where you are, than if you had your own
sweet will to-morrow. However grey and cheerless duty be, a man must trample down his moods
and do it. Then, in God's time, far sooner than
we dream, the richest joys will reach us unexpectedly, and life will unfold itself, out of the
mists, into a thing of beauty and a joy for ever.
He that believeth can say ' Get thee behind me,
Satan.' He that believeth will not make haste.

Again, I keep whispering this text within my
heart, when I observe our common haste to see
results. The man who believes in himself and in
his message is never in a hurry to see results.
The army general who cannot trust himself grows
feverish for some brilliant deed of arms. But
Lord Kitchener will wait and plan and scheme
till the whole nation grows restless and impatient ;
he believes in himself, and he will not make
haste. It is always a mark of inferior capacity to
be in a feverish hurry to be recognised. No
genius ever goes to sleep with the wild hope that
to-morrow he may wake up famous. Genius is

sublimely confident and easy ; with the touch
of God-given power comes sweet assurance.
What I feel is that if the church of Christ
really believes in her mission and her message,
she must not be feverish about results.   I think
it is oftener faithlessness than faith that clamours
for immediate statistics.   The purposes of Heaven
are very long, and God fulfils Himself in many
ways.   The soul of man is infinitely delicate, and
you can never tabulate the powers that touch it.
Be not weary in well-doing.   You see no fruit ?
So be it.   Remember that with your covenanted
Lord a thousand years are as a single day.   He
that believeth is strong to sow in tears, but he
shall not make haste to reap in joy.

Now when we turn to the dealings of God
with men there is one thing that impresses us
very deeply.   It is the slowness of all God's
procedure in guiding and blessing our humanity.
God never hurries ; He moves with infinite ease.
He takes an age to perfect one of His thoughts
within us.   What I might call the leisureliness of
providence is written large on human history.
Think of the weary discipline of Israel till they
had grasped the mighty truth that God is one ;

remember how men had to wait for centuries
before the world was ready for Christ Jesus;
reflect that nineteen centuries have gone, and we
seem only to be touching the hem of Christ's
garment yet—and you will apprehend the leisureliness of heaven.   In all God's dealings with the
human race, and in all God's dealings with the
human soul, there is purpose, urgency, infinite
persistence ;   but I think no man will detect
hurry there.

Now take our text and let it illuminate that
thought.   It is because God believes in man that
He refuses to hurry his development.   If there
were no potentiality in human nature, no promise
of a divine ideal at its core, a single season might
be enough to ripen it, as it ripens the corn that
rustles in the field.   There are creatures that
dance and die all in one summer's evening; and
a summer's evening is long enough for them.
But a thousand evenings are not enough for
man, there is such promise in the sorriest life.
When I think how long a little child is helpless,
absolutely dependent on another's love ; when I
think of the slow stages of our growth up the
steep slope to moral and spiritual manhood ; when

I remember that every vision that beckons us, and every hope that fires us, and every truth that illuminates and saves us, was won out of the riches of God, through the discipline and the chastisement of ages, I feel that the belief of God in man is wonderful : He hath believed in us, and therefore hath made no haste. We speak a great deal about our faith in God. Never forget God's glorious faith in us.

And when I pass to the earthly life of Jesus, I am arrested by the same procedure there. He was leisurely, just because He trusted men. He did not despair of them when they were backward ; He did not reject them because they were slow to learn. When He had chosen a heart, He trained it with infinite patience, and just because He believed in it, He would not hurry. Compare His treatment of Judas with that of Peter. Christ did not believe in the sincerity of Judas. He knew him to be a hypocrite, and a traitor, and 'what thou doest do quickly'—haste ! get done with it ! But Peter ! Christ thoroughly believed in Peter. He saw the possibilities in Peter. He knew that underneath the sand, driven by the wind. there was bed-rock to build a church upon.

So Peter was allowed to go out into the night,
and to weep bitter tears under the look of Christ.
There was no hurry.   Let him weep his eyes out.
Jesus believed in Peter, and let him alone.   And
Jesus was scourged and hung upon the cross, and
lay in the grave, and rose on the third day, and
the hours seemed endless to the fallen disciple,
yet never a word of comfort came from his Lord.
Then at long last, 'Simon, son of Jonas, lovest
thou Me ?'   'Yea, Lord, Thou knowest that I
love Thee.'   The wheels of the chariot of Christ
had tarried, just because He trusted that great
heart.

And so we come back to where we started
from—the freedom from feverishness that is a
mark of faith.   Do you believe ?   Then the
peace that passes understanding shall keep your
heart and mind through Jesus Christ.   Do you
believe—but let me use a little illustration that
may help to make clearer what I mean.

I notice that in these flimsy tenements which
are being run up in various quarters of the city,
there is a great hurry to get all finished by the
term.   There is a feverish eagerness apparent to
have everything ready and complete by Whitsun-

day. But the old cathedrals were not built that way. The old cathedrals took hundreds of years to build. Men lived and died, and handed on the work, and there was plenty of time, for was not the work God's? And every finial and turret was perfected, for the builders said the 'eyes of God were there.' Are ye not temples of the living God? Shall not the work go on through all eternity? Be zealous, strenuous! Give thy whole heart to things! But he that believeth shall not make haste.

THE OPENED WINDOWS

His windows being open in his chamber toward Jerusalem.—
Daniel vi. 10.

IT was in an hour of very sore distress that
Daniel acted in the manner of which our text
speaks. The crisis had come which he had long
expected, and the crisis drove him to the feet of
God. In the years that immediately preceded
the Scottish Reformation, there was one thing
that rankled in the breast of all true Scotsmen.
It was the presence and the power of Frenchmen
in almost all the high offices of state in Scotland.
In much the same way there was widespread
irritation, rising at times into very bitter envy,
among the aristocratic patriots of Babylon at the
powerful eminence of foreigners like Daniel. In
Scotland, David Rizzio was assassinated ; but
Babylon was more advanced in civilisation than
Scotland. The presidents and the princes and
the counsellors took a more politic way of accom-

plishing their designs. Men were forbidden to pray for thirty days. They must ask no petition of any God or man, save of Darius. And it was then, when the royal decree was signed, and when Daniel fully recognised his peril, that he went into his house to pray, his windows being open toward Jerusalem.

So much for the historical setting of the words. Now, bringing them into a larger environment, I find that they carry three suggestions. The first is the moral significance of indifferent actions. The second is the true relationship of the unseen and the seen. The third is the right attitude towards the unattainable. Allow me to dwell on each for a few moments.

First, then, whenever I think of Daniel's procedure, it reminds me of the moral significance of indifferent actions. There was nothing remarkable in ‚opening a window. It is one of those common acts which we do without a thought. The Babylonian slaves in Daniel's house would not attach the slightest importance to it. Yet, every time that Daniel opened that lattice, it spoke of a heart that was travelling to Jerusalem. It was the index of a soul that in seductive

Babylon was true to the God and the Temple of its race. It revealed a spirit which honours could not destroy; a love which distance was powerless to quench; a heroism which no impending doom could shake. The action in itself was immaterial, but we see how full of significance it was.

There is another verse in the Old Testament that I should like you to note in connection with our text. I read in Genesis that when Abram and Lot parted, Lot pitched his tent towards Sodom (xiii. 12). There was no fault to be found with the actual place of pitching ; it was just like a hundred other scenes of bivouac. There was good pasture for the weary flocks, a brook to wash off the soiling of the day, and sufficient shelter from the keen night winds. Viewed in itself, the choice was immaterial. It was like the opening and closing of a lattice. The moral significance lies in the word toward— Lot pitched his tent that night *toward* Sodom. It was the direction, not the place, that was important. It was the trend of the journey, not the actual pitch. Had Lot been travelling away from Sodom, the site would presumably have been ideal.   But Daniel opened his windows toward Jerusalem, and so doing revealed a heart true to the highest.   Lot pitched his tent toward Sodom, and the tragedy lay in the direction.

The truth, then, which I wish to impress on you is this, that there are actions which are quite indifferent in themselves, and which in themselves, when viewed in isolation, may have no moral importance whatsoever; and yet if they reveal the trend of character, and the direction that our thoughts and wishes and feelings are setting in, no man dare say that they are immaterial.   It is not the actual achievement of my life, it is my life's direction that is of supreme importance; and as the handful of grass thrown up into the wind will tell whence the wind comes and whither it is going, and as the straw will show which way the current runs, so deeds, intrinsically insignificant, may be big with meaning, if they disclose the movement of a life.   There are some things that are always and everywhere right. There are other things that in all circumstances are wrong.   It is impossible to conceive a state of being, for instance, in which falsehood should be a virtue or bravery a vice.   But in between

these everlasting fixities, there lies a whole world
of endeavour and of action, and the moral value
of the action is determined by the trend and
purpose of the underlying character. A score of
lattices might be flung wide in Babylon, and
might indicate nothing save that the heat was
lessening. But the lattice of Daniel, open toward
Jerusalem, was the witness of an heroic heart.
And a score of tents might be pitched in the
plains where Lot was, and might mean no more
than that the pasturage was good. But the tent
of Lot, pitched there towards Sodom, told of a
character hurrying to ruin.

I read the other day a characteristic anecdote
about Professor Faraday. The lecture was over,
and he was leaving the class-room, when some
little article dropped from his hand on the floor.
The Professor searched for it, but it was nowhere
to be found; it is extraordinary how things will
hide themselves on a level floor. And one of
his students who was with him said, 'Never
mind, sir, it is of no consequence whether we
find it to-night or no.' 'That is quite true,'
said the Professor, 'but it is of the gravest consequence to me that I be not baffled in my

determination to find it'—he knew the moral value of such actions. We are all too ready to say, 'It does not matter.' We are too fond of thinking, 'What's the harm?' We isolate our actions, view them abstractly, judge them by inexorable codes of right and wrong. But the man who is in earnest about moral excellence will never forget the complexity of character; he will feel that what for other men is harmless, for him may be a step towards degradation. The supreme question is whither is he tending—is it towards Sodom or is it towards Jerusalem?

In the second place, I catch a glimpse in our text of the true relationship of the unseen and the seen.

When Daniel opened his window, as his custom was, it was not Babylon that he desired to see : his heart was far away in his own country. Just as the Scottish emigrant in Canada dreams of the mountains and moors where he was born, and sees the glen again, and the burn swollen with the rain, and the dripping bracken, and the glory of purple heather : so Daniel in exile, heartsick if not homesick, craved for the land and the Temple that he loved. He could not see them ; they were beyond his vision. It would bring them no nearer to fling wide the lattice. Yet an instinct that every one of us can understand moved him to open the window towards Jerusalem. He could brook no barrier betwixt him and the unseen.

And then, what happened when the window was opened? Why, the life in Babylon broke in on Daniel noisily. It had been dulled and deadened and indistinct before; but now it rolled like a tide into the room. He heard the wagon labouring through the street, and the wagoners shouting in their upland dialect. He heard the angry chaffering in the market, and the voices of children romping in the squares. He saw the aged resting in the shadow, and the mothers with their infants in their arms. And now a soldier, and now a laden country-woman, and now a beggar, and now a Chaldean priest, passed by under the open lattice. It was not to see all this that Daniel opened his window. His window was open to the unseen Jerusalem. But in the very instant of his opening it so, the life around him became doubly real.

Now that is like a little parable of something

that happens to the truly religious man.   Let him open the window of his heart on the unseen, and the life at his door grows doubly real to him.   It is not true that a heart-hunger for the unseen robs the life round us of its charm and import. The surging and strange life of common streets, the crooning of motherhood, the song of children, are touched into meanings hitherto undreamed of, when the lattice of the soul is opened Christwards. When the gaze of the heart is towards its unseen Saviour, then do we love, because He first loved us.   And slowly but surely, kindled by love's insight, there grows the vision of the worth of life.   We cannot despise men for whom Jesus lived.   We cannot scorn men for whom Jesus died.   We cannot be indifferent to human suffering, when we remember the compassion of the Saviour.   We cannot think lightly of motherhood or childhood, when we recall the home at Nazareth.   The life in the street, so coloured and so changeful ; and the life in the cottage, with its joy and pain ; childhood and age, suffering and sorrow—all are enriched and illumined and transfigured, when the soul's window is opened toward Jerusalem.

There is no such instance in history of this as the life of Jesus Christ Himself. He is the peerless example of that true relationship that is suggested to us by the text. He lived and moved among eternal things. He enjoyed unbroken fellowship with God. His heart was in heaven where His Father dwelt, as truly as the heart of Daniel was in Jerusalem. Yet, though all the windows of His soul were opened heavenward, the life around Him was infinitely precious ; the meanest villager ceased to be insignificant, to a heart whose lattice was thrown wide on God. He could not disown the woman at the well ; He dare not spurn the woman who was a sinner. He was moved with compassion for the widow of Nain, and he wept before the grave of Lazarus. There was never an anger like the anger of Jesus ; there was never a pity so resourceful and so strong. No man could charge our Lord with other-worldliness. His vision of God was no ecstatic rapture. All things around Him were more real and near, because the window was open toward Jerusalem.

Lastly, and very briefly, our text suggests the right attitude towards the unattainable. Daniel had thriven very well in exile, and had risen to quite remarkable power ; but chains are still chains however they be gilded, and Daniel was a prisoner in Babylon. He would never again cross the fords of Jordan, nor ever look upon the Holy City. His prospects of return were hopeless ; he was doomed to a perpetual separation. Yet, though all hope of seeing Jerusalem was banished, we read that he opened his windows toward Jerusalem, and that suggests to me the right attitude towards the unattainable.

For every man, who is striving to live nobly, is struggling after things he cannot reach. He has his Jerusalem, but it is far away, and he knows that on this side of the grave he will not see it. Dimly, and as in the mystical distance, he has grown conscious of an ideal character ; but the failure and the flaw of every day, and the recurrent weakness, and the unbridled heart, tell him too plainly that he is far off from it. It is when we feel that deeply that we are tempted to despair. It is in such hours that we fall to lower levels. We grow heartsick ; we shall never see Jerusalem ; let us be contented with our little room. But, I say to you, dare to be a Daniel.

Fling wide the lattice towards what you can never reach. Have the casement open towards the unattainable ; and by the open casement be in prayer. And though the love and purity you long for, and all the depth and strength of perfect character be as far distant from your hungry heart as Judea from the yearning heart of Daniel, yet in the very craving lies nobility, and the pledge of attainment in the tearless morn. Daniel to-day, in the sunshine and love of God, in the land where they fear no death, and need no Temple, possesses and enjoys all that he craved for once,—when he opened his windows toward Jerusalem.

IS LIFE A TRAGEDY?

At a meeting of our Literary Society on Tuesday night, a young man read an essay on the Tragedy of Life. I did not hear the essay, but I gathered from the subsequent discussion, which I did hear, that it was an able paper. Now there was one thing in that discussion which impressed me very much. One speaker remarked that in the essay there had been no reference to Jesus Christ. The essayist replied that if the minister was doing his duty in the pulpit, that argument should be familiar to them all. I thought the whole discussion very significant of the trend and the temper of these present times. And I should like therefore to speak for a little on what the writer called Life's Tragedy, viewed from the standpoint of Christ Jesus.

Now we all admit that there are tragedies in life. We cannot live very long without observing that. What does impress us as our life advances

is how men try to conceal the tragedies, and
how the secret breaks through all disguise, and
gets written out so that he who runs may
read. It is thus that we grow more charitable
with the years. We learn to read the signs
of the times more fluently. We might have
been bitter, too, had we had *that* to bear
It is so easy to be unkind, when we are unhappy.

But it is one thing to say that life has tragedies
and another to talk of the tragedy of life. The
depths of the heavens may be of cloudless azure,
though thunderous clouds are moving in the sky.
What then is tragedy? It is a play, or drama,
that marches with stately movement to calamity.
Dante called his great epic a comedy because it
closed in the glorious vision of God. But in
tragedy the characters move onward, through
love, and hate, and the passions of joy and
sorrow, to an end that is shadowed, and an
issue that is dark ; and when above the characters is seen the hand of Fate, moving them
irresistibly to their doom, then we have tragedy
in the full meaning of the term. When men
speak of the tragedy of life, I take it that that

is exactly what they mean. No one denies
that life has exquisite joys. No one denies that
there are days of sunshine, seasons when all the
trees in the forest clap their hands. But if life
is tragedy, its ultimate end is darkness ; the play
is progressing sorrow-ward, not joyward. We
have to cross the bar into the boundless deep,
but we dare not hope to see our Pilot there. No
matter what the struggle and the strain, life is not
tragedy if the end be happy. It is only when
we believe that human life is moving towards a
climax of unhappiness, that we can talk of the
tragedy of life.

Now the mood or temper which interprets the
world so goes by the familiar name of pessimism.
A pessimist is one who says life is a tragedy.
And I call pessimism a mood or temper because
it reveals itself in every human activity. It bursts
out into poetry in Byron. It creeps into politics
under the name of Nihilism. It becomes a religion
in the great creed of Buddha. It has its philosophers in men like Schopenhauer. Had you
asked Byron what he thought of life, he would
have answered that for all its glories it was
tragedy. If you travelled to the dreamy East

and asked the Buddhist what he thought of life, he too would tell you that human life is tragedy, and that the great aim of life is to get rid of selfhood. Millions believe, then, that life is a tragedy, and all who believe that, we call pessimists.

And I think it is one marked feature of to-day that that mood has crept into our popular literature. The pessimistic spirit has been popularised in a way that the world has never seen before. I do not forget that the consummate masters have never accepted that gospel of despair. I do not forget the magnificent faith of Browning, nor the quiet and luminous hope of Tennyson, though even Tennyson, as his life advanced, seems to have lost some of his strong assurance. But the fact remains that the plays and novels and stories that are greedily devoured by hundreds of thousands to-day are largely tinged with the pessimistic temper. Once, a novel would hardly have been called a novel, unless it closed with the ringing of marriage bells. But now it is quite allowable to close with the blighting of hope in a wild and stormy sunset. The belief that life for all its effort is but tragedy, that the world is hurrying

forward to the dark, that man is the powerless
instrument of fate, a helpless pawn on the chess-
board of the universe—this thought, subtly and
stealthily, is finding its way into the hearts of
thousands in the leisure hours they give to lighter
reading.

Now I wonder if we can explain at all the
prevalence of this pessimistic temper. I think
there are three things that help us to account
for it.

Firstly, there is a very noble reason. It is that
we take life very seriously now. We are all interested in the great social problems, and that has
opened our eyes to the miseries abroad. It was
all very well for the poet Pope, for instance, to
pen that famous line, 'Whatever is, is right.'
But that was the optimism of ignorance, not of
knowledge, the faith of an age that shut its eyes
to facts ; and I think a recoil from that was quite
inevitable : brave hearts were bound to rise up
and deny it. Depend upon it, that if one century
says 'Whatever is, is right,' the next century
will take its own revenge and say 'Whatever is,
is wrong.' The world advances as the pendulum
swings, and through extremes we come to the

mean at last. I think, then, there is something
noble in our pessimism. It at least means that we
have begun to see and feel. We are taking life
so seriously now, and we are feeling the pressure
of its burden so, that the shallow optimist who
refuses to face facts is out of date by half a
century.

But then again this is a time of contrasts, and
a time of sharp contrasts is almost always pessimistic. It is when class is separated from class,
that men begin to feel the hopelessness of things.
In a little village you rarely find a pessimist ;
the lawyer and the cobbler are too good friends
for that. I mean that the rich are not so very
rich, and the poor are not so very poor ; they
mix and mingle in a common brotherhood,
and there is nothing like that for keeping the
heart sweet. But it is not village-life that is
prominent to-day. It is the life of the great and
crowded city. And in a city the rich are a great
deal richer, and the poor in a score of senses are
far poorer ; and the separation and conflict inevitably engendered carry the iron into innumerable
souls. Our modern pessimism is not the child of
the country. There is no glory of the Highland

heather in it ; no music of the burn, nor any
lilt of birds.   It is the child of the city, that
place of glaring contrasts, of downcrushing, of
seething discontent.   It is there that men speak
of the tragedy of life.

But perhaps there is a deeper reason still.
I refer to the materialism that is current.   There
is a strong tendency abroad that meets us constantly, to explain man in terms of force and
matter.   In some quarters the great thought of
evolution has been pushed so far, and the doctrine
of heredity has been so strained, that man is
practically an automaton, and what we call free-
will .a sweet delusion.   Such teaching is but
fatalism in disguise.   It is John Calvin without
the grace of God.   And Calvinism with God's
grace was stern enough ; but without it, it is
the nursing-mother of despair.   If I thought
there was no reality in my free-will, I should
become a pessimist to-morrow.   If I am only
impelled towards the inevitable by the pressure of the long past that is within me, life
immediately becomes a tragedy for me.   And
I doubt not that it is some dim sense of that,
moving in what is called the spirit of the age,

that gives what I have named the pessimistic note to so many books that are being widely read.

Now (and I speak with reverence and adoration and under a deep sense of what I owe to Christ), if there ever was a man in history who had ample cause to be a pessimist, I think it was our Saviour Jesus Christ. Whatever life may be for you and me, life was no sweet paradise for Him ; and if all experience was summed up in His experience, He had some right to talk of the tragedy of life. He was filled with the passion to love and to serve His fellows, yet they cried 'Crucify Him, crucify Him! Not this man, but Barabbas.' From the hour of His baptism, right along all His ministry, there lay the shadow of the cross to come. A tragedy moves with lofty march towards calamity. Christ moved with supreme nobility to Calvary. Shall *He* not talk of the tragedy of life ?

Instead of that, Christ talked about His joy ; He looked facts in the face and yet was joyful. Instead of that, Christ talked about His peace ; a peace that passed all understanding filled His

heart. But, most significant of all, He turned to
men and said, 'I am come that they might have
life and might have it more abundantly.' This,
then, was the very object of Christ's coming ;
that men might enjoy a larger measure of life.
Had life been a tragedy to Jesus Christ, I do
not think He would have wished to add to it.
Buddha looked out on life and saw its sorrow ;
and he said, 'Life is a tragedy, let us get done
with it.' But Jesus looked out on life, saw all
its sorrow, and felt it with an intensity Buddha
never knew, and yet in the face of it all He
dared to say, 'I am come that the world might
have more abundant life.' The question is, can
we discover the sources of this amazing optimism
of Jesus ? I wish to indicate one or two of them
and so close.

Well, in the first place, Christ was supremely
certain that His Father was present and working
in the world. Above all sorrow and sin, and
struggle and failure, Christ felt the pressure of a
sovereign power, and the movement of the infinite love of heaven. In the Old Testament
men had descried God's sovereignty, but it was
an awful and tremendous sovereignty. With

Jesus it has become a much more gentle attribute ; it clothes the grass and sees the sparrow
fall. You remember the famous line of Robert
Browning, 'God's in His heaven, all's right with
the world'? That was one source of the optimism
of Browning ; but the optimism of Jesus went a
great deal deeper. It was the fact that God was
in His *earth*, so that the ravens were fed and the
lilies were adorned, and so that the very hairs
of a man's head are numbered—it was that which
gave a radiant quietude to Christ.

Then Jesus believed, with a faith that was
magnificent, in the freedom and the worth of
personality, and whenever a man comes to
believe in that, it is impossible to hold that life
is a tragedy. How tenderly and skilfully Jesus
dealt with men !—it is clear that every man was a
new problem to Him. Were manhood forged and
fashioned by resistless influences, Christ would have
dealt with men upon the scale of the hundred ;
but Christ never dealt upon the scale of hundreds,
Christ always dealt upon the scale of one. That
means that personality is real. That means that
every life is a new thing. That means that in
the worst there is some possibility that can be

touched by love and become conquering. And
it was that faith burning in the heart of Jesus
like a flame, which kept Him so calm and hopeful
in the world.

Then never forget that Jesus believed in
heaven ; He launched life out on to an endless
course. There may be many tears in the first
act of the play, but it is too soon yet to say
it is a tragedy. Who knows but that the master
brain which planned the drama may be going
to lead the action into sunlight? I can
understand a man being a pessimist, if he really
believes that death is the end of all. The pessimist would have a strong case against the
Almighty, if the individual perished at the
grave. But if beyond that there is eternal life,
with its never-ending expansion of the soul, I
think it well to suspend judgment for a little.
We shall not lose our individuality in heaven—
' In My Father's house are many mansions.' And
we shall certainly not cease to work ; heaven
is the joy of the Lord, and the Lord is never
idle. All we have striven to be shall become
possible. All that we tried to do shall meet us
there. The cravings for better things we could

not realise, the longings that stirred us though never a man knew of them, shall be the first angels to kiss us in the glory. In the mighty conception of that eternal destiny, time ceased to be a tragedy for Christ.

TO THE HALF-HEARTED

Whatsoever ye do, do it heartily, as to the Lord.—Col. iii. 23.

I WANT you to note how our text is introduced ; it has a very suggestive and illuminative context. ' Servants, obey in all things your masters according to the flesh,' that is verse twenty-two ; and then, ' Whatsoever ye do, do it heartily, as to the Lord,' that is verse twenty-three. Now the servants of whom Paul speaks in verse twenty-two are not domestic servants in our sense. They were slaves, bought for a little money ; the property and the chattels of their master. Yet even to slaves, who got no wages and who had no rights, clear and imperious comes the command of God, ' Whatsoever ye do, do it heartily.'

Now I think that is very suggestive for to-day. I can hardly talk to a master-painter or a master-baker, but I hear complaints about the degeneracy of labour. Men are not faithful, they have to be watched like children ; the loyal

service of an older day is dead. So say the
masters ; and on the other hand the men say
that had they a more direct interest in their work,
and a more immediate concern in its prosperity,
they would throw themselves into it with doubled
zeal. Now all that may be true. But the point
is that if the Bible holds, and if this text be really
the word of God, nothing on earth, not even the
worst relationships of capital and labour, can ever
excuse half-hearted work. Your hours are long ?
—so were those of the Colossian slaves. Your
pay is poor?—the Colossian slave had none.
Your mistress is tyrannical and mean ?—but the
Colossian mistress lashed her servants. Yet
whatsoever ye do, ye slaves, cries Paul, do it all
heartily as to the Lord.

I want you to note, too, that this text was
never better illustrated than in the life of the
man who was inspired to pen it. There was an
enthusiasm and a concentration about Paul, which
have won the admiration of all time. ' One thing
I do, forgetting the things that are behind, I
press towards the mark,' says the apostle ; and
whatsoever he did, he did it heartily, as unto
the Lord who loved him so. It is so easy to

preach and never intend to practise. It is so hard
to practise first, and then to preach. It gives
a wonderful power to our text, and charges its
mandate with redoubled urgency, when we remember who the writer was. Men have brought
many charges against Paul, but I do not think
his bitterest enemy has ever charged him with
half-heartedness. There is a glow and fervour
in the man that marks in an instant the divine
enthusiast. Others might waver, Paul battled to
his goal. Others might yield, Paul was invincible.
And had you seen him working at his tentmaking,
in the late night when the city was asleep, you
would have found him plying the tentmaker's
needle, and singing, I doubt not, as in the prison
at Philippi, with the very heartiness and zeal that
filled his preaching of Christ crucified.

It is, then, of this whole-heartedness, of this
fine concentration or enthusiasm, that I want to
speak a little to-night. And I should like to say,
by way of caution, that true enthusiasm is not a
noisy thing. Whenever we think of an enthusiastic crowd, we think of uproar, tumult, wild
excitement. And I grant you that in the life of
congregated thousands, touched into unity by

some great emotion, there seems to be some call
for loud expression. But just as there is a sorrow
that lies too deep for tears, there is an enthusiasm
far too deep for words ; and the intense purpose
of the whole-hearted man is never noisy. When
the children of Israel, defeated by the Philistines,
sent for the ark of God into the camp, do you
remember how, when the ark appeared, they
shouted till the earth rang and rent? Yet spite
of that effervescence of emotion they were defeated, and the ark of God was captured. But
Jesus, in the enthusiasm of His kingly heart,
set His face steadfastly to go to Jerusalem ; and
yet He would not strive nor cry nor lift up His
voice in the streets. The noisiest are generally
shallow. There is a certain silence, as of an
under-purpose, wherever a man is working
heartily.

> ' Prune thou thy words, thy thoughts control
>   That o'er thee swell and throng ;
>   They shall condense within thy soul
>   And change to purpose strong.'

Whole-heartedness, then, is never a noisy virtue ;
and I have thought it right to dwell on that,
that we may be on our guard against its counter-

feits.   But if it be not noisy, this at least is true
of it : it is one condition of the best success.
The chairman of the Congregational Union of
Scotland, in an address he delivered some time
ago at Glasgow, told us that a friend had met
him lately, and said to him, 'I suppose you
have heard that Mr. So-and-so has failed?' The
chairman had not heard it.   'Well he has,' said
his friend, 'and little wonder, for he starved his
business.   He did not even put *himself* into it.'
He did not put himself into the work ; he did
not do it heartily as to the Lord.   And could we
trace the history of failure—that long, sad story
of the world—I think we should find that for
one who went to the wall through want of intellect, there were a score who reached that pass
through want of heart.   To concentrate, as all
the apostles did ; to have the resolute enthusiasm
of Jesus, *that* spirit has something congenial to
success in it ; and I use success in its best and
noblest senses, some of which the world might
call defeat.

But the virtue of whole-heartedness is more than
that.   It is one of the conditions of the truest
happiness.   There comes a certain joy as of the

morning, a certain zest and buoyancy of spirit,
when whatsoever we do is lone heartily, as to
the Lord.   When we are ha f-hearted, the hours
have leaden feet.   We becon e fretful, easily pro-
voked ; the very grasshopper becomes a burden.
But when, subduing feeling, we turn with our
whole energy of soul to grapple with our duty or
with our cross, it is wonderful how under the long
shadows we hear unexpectedly a sound of music.
To be half-hearted is to be half-happy.   It is to
live in a lack-lustre kind of way.   And so it is
to live in an un-Christlike way, it is to know
little of the joy of Jesus.   Do you not think the
joy of Jesus Christ was linked, far down, with
His whole-hearted service ?   He never could
have spoken of His joy but for His unswerving
fidelity to God.   And when at last upon the
cross there rang out the loud, glad cry, ' It is
finished,' there was joy in it because the stupen-
dous work of saving men had been carried
through to its triumph and its crown.

And there can be little question that the more
heartily we do our humble duty, the more we
feel we are doing it for God.   It is one of the
secrets for bringing heaven near us, for feeling

the Infinite with us and within us, to be whole-
hearted in the present task. Thinkers have often
noted this strange fact: that great enthusiasms
tend to become religious. Let a man be mastered
by any great idea, and sooner or later he will find
the shadow of God on it. But that is true not
of great enthusiasms alone; it holds of whole-
heartedness in every sphere. When Luther said,
'Laborare est orare'—to labour is to pray—you
may be sure that that great soul did not mean
that work could ever take the place of prayer.
He knew too well the value of devotion, and the
blessed uplifting of the quiet hour with God, ever
to think that toil could take its place. But just
as in earnest prayer the heavens are opened to us,
and we are led into the presence and glory of the
King, so in our earnest and whole-hearted toil,
clouds scatter, the mists of feelings and passions
are dispelled, and we are led into a peace and
strength and sweet detachment without which no
man shall see the Lord. It is in that sense that
to labour is to pray. To be whole-hearted is to
be facing heavenward. And the great loss of all
half-hearted men and women is this, that above
the dust, and the stress and strain of life, above

the fret and weariness of things, they catch no
glimpse of the eternal purpose, nor of the love,
nor of the joy of God.

Indeed, if that old saying ' like to like ' be true,
the men who are half-hearted must be blind.
For if there is one demonstrable fact, I think it
is this : we are the creatures of a whole-hearted
God. When I remember the thoroughness of
the Creator's workmanship ; when I think of the
consummate genius and care that He has lavished
on the tiniest weed ; when I recall the age-long
discipline that was preparing the world for Jesus
Christ ; I feel that the heart of God is in His
work. And I feel, too, that if my heart is not in
mine, I must be out of touch with the Creator.
The gods of savages are generally lazy, because
the savages themselves are lazy, and they have
spiritual sense enough to know that there cannot
be communion without kinship. But our God
is the infinite Creator ; the master-builder, the
thorough and perfect workman. And I know
not how a half-hearted servant can have any
kinship with a whole-hearted Lord. O brother,
whatsoever ye do, do it heartily, that you may
come into line with the eternal. It is the pity of

all half-hearted men that they are out of harmony with God.

One other word on our text and I have done. I want you to note how the writer lays his hand on the real secret of all the large enthusiasms. He centres his appeal upon a person. Had Paul been writing in some quiet academy, the text, I dare say, might have read like this, ' Whatsoever ye do, do it heartily, for that is the road to nobility of character'; or ' Whatsoever ye do, do it heartily, for the best work is always done that way.' But Paul did not write in any quiet academy. Paul wrote for the masses. Paul wrote for the great world. And he knew that nothing abstract, nothing cold, would ever inspire the enthusiasm of thousands. A cause must be concentrated in some powerful name, it must live in the flesh and blood of personality, if the hearts of the many are ever to be stirred, and the lives of the many are ever to be won. So Paul, with the true instinct of universal genius, gathered all abstract arguments for zeal into the living argument of Jesus. And whatsoever ye do, do it heartily, as what? *as to the Lord.*

And so by the roundabout road of this address,

you see I have brought you back to the feet of Christ, and wherever on these summer evenings we may start from, I trust always to leave you there. I believe that the secret of all noble living lies in the company of Jesus Christ.   And for making us earnest, thorough, quietly resolute, no matter what fickleness or cowardice we start with, there is really nothing like fellowship with Him. Do you want to be truer?   Get a little closer. Are you ashamed of your half-heartedness? Get nearer. Then back to your work again, alone yet not alone: for the time flies, and eternity is near, and you shall pass this way but once.

THE UNLIKELY INSTRUMENTS
OF GOD

Babylon hath been a golden cup in the Lord's hand.—Jer. li. 7.

IF there was one city in the world that seemed to be independent, it was that city of Babylon. It was magnificent in its equipments, ruled with consummate ability, strong with the most powerful army of the time. It worshipped its own gods, and was contented with them; it had nothing but scorn for the poor deities of Israel. Its cup *was* golden, there was no doubt of it. There was not a boy playing about its avenues but would have cried, 'The cup of our city hath been a golden cup!' But the prophet, inspired, saw that there was a Hand grasping the cup. 'Babylon hath been a golden cup in the Lord's hand.' It was golden, but for all that it was God's. It was He who had raised it up; it was He who held it; it was He who would hurl it, violently, to the ground.

Babylon, then, for all its power and all its independence, was an instrument of God, and no one can deeply study the word of God without coming to perceive the awful emphasis that it lays on the fact of instrumentality. The Bible, like Shakespeare, and yet in a sense far from Shakespeare's, seems to have stamped on it ' All the world's a stage, and all the men and women merely players.' We are not isolated ; we are not independent. We are not drifting, rudderless, on shadowy seas. Somehow, mysteriously, to an end we cannot see, and under a Providence that never errs, we all are instruments. Even Babylon is a golden cup in the Lord's hand.

This view of life fills all the Scripture, and if I thought we really knew the Scripture, it would be enough to indicate it and pass on. But are we truly studying the Word of God? Can we name, for instance, the conqueror of whom God said, ' Thou art my battleaxe ' ? Or the tyrant of whom God said, ' Thou art my servant '? God says to Cyrus, Thou art my battleaxe ; God says to Nebuchadnezzar, Thou art my servant. These men were strangers to the promises, bow-

ing in worship to the gods of heathendom; yet
'thou art *My* battleaxe, Cyrus'; 'thou art *My*
servant'—they were all the instruments of
Almighty God.

I learn, then, that beyond the sphere of grace
stretches the wide sphere of instrumentality.
Outside the hearts that have been touched to
holiness and won to the feet of the Lord Jesus
Christ, God has ten thousand instruments at
work. They do not know it—Babylon did not
know it. Why rage the heathen and imagine
vain things? They do not know it—Cyrus did
not know it. He battled, but never dreamed he
was God's battleaxe. So brains are scheming,
statesmen are plotting, armies are marching and
camping in the world; and you and I, taught in
the things of Scripture, are going to feel that
God is in it all. It was the prophet's outlook on
the world. We want the prophet's vision in
these times. We are summoned to think that all
that is meant by Babylon is a golden cup in the
Lord's hand.

Now sometimes the blindest eye can see how
exquisitely the instruments of God are fitted to
the task God has in hand. We feel that infinite

wisdom is at work, the tool has been chosen by a master-hand. In the story of our own country, for example, go back for a moment to Reformation times, and remember that Scotland was a feudal country, a land where kinship and blood and birth meant everything. Then think of the exquisite choice of God in the first preacher and martyr for the truth. The blood of kings was in the veins of Patrick Hamilton ; the greatest in the land were kin to him ; and that gave an impulse to the gospel of Jesus Christ that would have been wanting had Hamilton been base-born. There, in the story of our own dear country, is an example of the perfect choice of God. And there is not a land, and not a life, but could give signal instances like that.

But is not the general rule the very opposite ? I think it is the reverse that strikes us most. Here or there starts up some striking instance that reveals the perfect wisdom of God's choices. But far more often we are arrested differently ; we are staggered by the very strangeness of God's instruments. He is using means we never thought He would employ ; He is using the last men we should have dreamed of. We are face to face in the whole sweep of history with the unlikely instruments of God.

Think, for example, of the instrument which He used to keep alive the knowledge of His name. A man could not do it, it required a nation ; God's name is too great for one man to hold in trust; but of all the unlikely nations in the world, I think Israel was the most unlikely. What! shall the vivifying truth of all the ages be committed to a horde of slaves in Egypt ? Is it these men gathering the stubble yonder, and crying out under the taskmaster's lash—is it they who are to guard the knowledge of God that is to be crowned in the great gift of a Redeemer? To a human eye that seems the worst of choices, and yet that nation was the chosen of God. Israel became the instrument of Heaven. It was Israel that was the cradle of the Christ. Through wandering and war, through storm and sunshine, she was shaped and polished for most exalted use. Surely a most unlikely instrument, but for all that the instrument of God.

In other spheres, too, and in other ways, the same thing constantly meets us in the Bible.

Whenever I think of God's unlikely instruments, I think of little Samuel in the temple. You remember the message which God had to announce? A message of doom on Eli and his house. A dark, dread curse, hurled from the eternal throne at the wicked family of a weakly father. And who shall God choose to bear that message of woe? Some heart of iron? Some prophet like the Baptist? God chose a little child to be His instrument. Ah, what rebukes a little child can give! for they all live in the Temple, do they not? What sudden reproaches in their artless questionings! What censures and smitings of conscience in their innocence! A child may doom us. A little child shall lead us. It is one of God's unlikely instruments.

Now if Jesus of Nazareth be the Son of God, I shall expect to find Him adopting the same procedure. And Paul, in a passage of very lofty eloquence, has preached this doctrine of unlikely choices. For God, he says (and he is thinking of the Gospel), hath chosen the foolish things of the world to confound the wise ; and the weak things to confound those which are mighty ; and base things, yea the things that are not, to bring to naught the things that are. And what that means I cannot grasp or gather, unless this truth that I am trying to bring home had been burned into Paul's mind and heart. It is the wonder of heaven's choice of instruments for winning the triumphs of the Saviour's cause.

And tell me, has not the world wondered at it? It has been the perpetual marvel of the ages. I surmise from His very methods that Christ was Son of God, whenever I think of His choice of the disciples. Twelve men, provincial and unlettered—and all the world against them in the battle. The poetry of Greece, the arms of Rome, the institutions that had grown grey with time, the thought that had taken centuries to build, passions and vices, and the blight of atheism—that was the world, and against *all* the world, Peter and Andrew, and James and John, and Thomas. It was a strange choice, yet it was very Godlike. It was like the choice of the slaves in the fields of Egypt; like little Samuel against the hierarchy. Yet by such men, inspired by the Holy Ghost, victories were won that changed the world.

That, then, is the doctrine of unlikely instruments. Now every doctrine has its practical bearings. What, then, does that inexplicable feature of God's choice mean for you and me?

Well, first it guards us against putting limits upon God. Who shall dare say what powers may not be used by heaven, if even Babylon be a golden cup in the Lord's hand? We are so apt to have contracted views. We are so prone to think that God will only work by means of instruments we should have chosen, that when He contradicts us, and works in other ways, we are blind to the presence of the Divine in it. Give a wide sweep to sovereignty. Remember that His ways are not as ours. You think that He is coming in the whirlwind? Hark! He is whispering in the still small voice. You say that the winnowing-fan is in His hand, and behold, the bruised reed He will not break. That is the first use of God's unlikely instruments. It makes us watchful, open-hearted, very humble. We must be alive to possibilities of usefulness, or the chances are we may be missing God. Babylon, mother of harlots! drunk with the blood of the saints ! Out on thee, antichrist ! Yet Babylon hath been a golden cup in the Lord's hand.

And lastly, it should make us very strong when we are called to any little service. 'I am not fit for it ; I am the last man in the world for it '—quite right, my brother, probably you are ; but so was Israel, and the Lord called Israel ; and so was Samuel, and the Lord called Samuel : it is a kind of way God has of working. The men who think that they are fit for anything are very seldom fit for God's work. But the men who cry, as Jeremiah cried, ' Ah, Lord God, I am a child, and cannot speak '—it is such men whose lips are touched with fire, whose hearts are emboldened, and whose way is opened. For God is not bent on glorifying *you* ; God is bent on glorifying *Jesus*. And the more men see that the power is all of Him ; the more men feel, knowing your poor equipment, that this or that is the doing of the Lord, the greater the praise to an ascended Saviour. Let all the earth praise Him ! Worthy is the Lamb that was slain ! I take it that *that* is the deepest of all reasons for the unlikely instruments of God.

THE TOUCHSTONE OF FACT

Have ye not asked them that go by the way?—Job xxi. 29.

THE speaker of these words is Job, and it is not difficult to understand their fitness. Job is protesting against the shallow theories with which his friends had been trying to console him. Their view of providence was a singularly simple one. It would have been admirable, had it only been true. It was just that if a man is wicked he can never be prosperous, and if he is prosperous he cannot be wicked. Now Job had held that view himself once. He would not have quarrelled with it before his suffering. But when sorrow after sorrow fell on him, till his life was ruined and all his sky was dark, he was forced to look his old theories in the face. He learned that there were more mysteries abroad than he had ever dreamed of in his old philosophy. He saw that men who disowned and dishonoured God could be happy in their life and untroubled in their death. And he knew now that one might be earnestly devoted to the Highest, and yet might be beaten with the most cruel blows. And so he turns sharply here to his three friends, who were trying to console him with these discarded theories. Why have ye not asked them that go by the way : the men who go up and down the world with open eyes? They would have brought you home a store of facts that would have shattered your views of things to atoms. Job means that the providential theories of his three friends are worthless, because they are false to the observed facts of life.

Two thoughts, then, are suggested to me by this, and on these two I wish to dwell for a little. (1) The temptation to give little answers to great questions. (2) The duty of testing our theories by facts.

First, then : The temptation to give little answers to great questions.

There are some questions to the greatness of which we are blind, till they enter the circle of our own life-history—' he jests at scars who never felt a wound.' It was the wrecking of his home and the ruin of his hopes that set Job deeply pondering upon providence, and it was only then, in the hour of his own great sorrow, that he felt how terrible and vast was the problem. He had been quite contented with his little answers once. When the sun is shining it is sweet to have compact theories. But from the moment that the finger of God touched him, Job never gave, and Job never accepted, little answers to great questions again. The problem was wider than he had ever thought. God's ways were more intricate than he had dreamed. The justice of heaven in bestowing reward and punishment was not so evident as it seemed once. The little ready-made answers had been scattered, and Job was groping in the darkness now. It was exquisitely painful, but it was very blessed. It was the call of God to him to launch into the deep. Whatever else Job's suffering did for him, it banished his little answers to great questions.

And are we not saved from shallowness, as Job was, by the deeper and sterner experience of life? There is nothing like sorrow for testing a man's formulas, and if they are insufficient, for scattering them. Many a little answer has been banished, not by an argument, but by an illness. Many a system that seemed quite impregnable when tried and tested at the bar of logic, has simply crumbled into dust and ashes when the coffin was open and death was in the home.   Have ye not asked them that go by the way?   They have been through the deeps, and might have told you.   The world is too mysterious and awful to be explained by a few pious commonplaces.   Better be still, and know that He is God.   Clouds and darkness are around His throne.   Better than any glib answer to the problems, is to say with Christ, 'Father, Thy will be done.'

It has been noted as one of the great qualities of Shakespeare that he never yielded to this subtle temptation.   It is no idle flattery to say of him, that he saw life steadily and saw it whole.   He sent his heart out, up and down every way; he looked on all that men had dared and done and suffered, until the mysteries of life and love and death so overpowered him, that little answers died upon his lips.   'The thoughts of the wisest,' says the author of *Sesame and Lilies*, 'are but pertinent questions,' and I know no thoughts of which that is quite so true as the thoughts of the master-genius of our literature.   We come to Shakespeare as the three friends came to Job.   We have our little solutions all cut and dry. And Shakespeare turns on us, as Job turned on the three, and he says, ' What! have ye not asked them that go by the way ? ' And then he takes us out into life's way, and shows us such heights, such depths, such glories, and such sorrows, that the answers we should have given once are silenced ; it is all far more mysterious than we dreamed.

And the same thing, in infinitely nobler ways, meets me in the life of our Lord Jesus Christ. I think our Lord loved every little thing, with the one exception of a little answer. Men came to Him with the profoundest questions, about their souls, their duty, their judgment, or their heaven. What impresses me is that the profoundest question always elicited a profounder answer. ' Who is my neighbour ? ' He was asked that once ; and the reply was the parable of the Samaritan. Has not neighbourliness had a deeper meaning ever since ? ' Master, who did sin, this man or his parents, that he was born blind ? ' And the reply has lifted the problem to new levels, and been like a cordial to a thousand sufferers. ' Tell us,' said the disciples, ' when shall these things be ? ' And the reply of Jesus was sublime—'I cannot.' 'Of that day and that hour knoweth no man, no not the angels which are in heaven, neither the Son, but the Father.' It is the sublimest instance in all history, of the refusal to give a little answer.

And I am perfectly certain that much of the gospel's power in the world is to be found in a similar refusal. If the gospel of Christ appeals to men and women, and if its appeal has been powerful through the chance and change of time, one secret of its power has been this, that it has dared to give great answers to the great questions of the human heart. It is well to distrust solutions that solve everything. I had a professor in my university who made things so plain that we were all perplexed. There is something lacking in every creed and system that is too ready with universal answers. But the gospel has no easy explanations. It is *good* news, because it is *great* news. It says: 'The questions of the soul are mighty, and I shall furnish them with mighty answers.' You say to it, 'What must I do to be saved?' And does it bid you go and show some little kindnesses? It says, 'Believe on the Lord Jesus Christ, and thou shalt be saved,' and

belief is the whole manhood roused to heroism.
You say to it, 'What about my sin?' And
does it bid you be happy, and do the best you
can? It talks of Blood, and shows you a Saviour
crucified, and says, 'Though your sin be as
scarlet, it shall be white as snow'—and that
appeals to the very depths of me. Beware of
cheap and easy substitutes for Christ. They will
not last, they do not satisfy. Ask those who
have gone by the way whether they do. I have
a gospel I shall never be ashamed of, for it scorns
to give little answers to great questions.

The second thought suggested by our text is
the duty of testing our theories by facts.

This was the complaint of Job against his
friends; their views did not square with the
known facts of life. They had never really
tested their pet theories by the actual experience
of men and women. They were convinced that
if a man were righteous, he would prosper. And
they were equally convinced that when a man was
crushed to the earth, as Job was, it was the index
that heaven was angry with his sin. They had
been trained in this view of providential dealing,
and it had never occurred to them to question it.

But Job had found that their theories were inadequate. Taught by his own strange case, he had looked abroad, and had grappled boldly with the clear facts of life. And now he turns upon his would-be comforters, and charges them with shutting their eyes to facts. 'You have never asked those who go by the way,' he says. You have never brought your clear-cut doctrine to the touchstone of the experience of men. Job had been wakened to the great duty of testing his theories by facts.

And is not the progress of Job through his great agony a parable of the progress of the human race? Like Job's three friends, we all start with mistakes, and in bringing these to the touchstone of reality lies one great measure of our moral advance. The savage believes that the sun moves round the earth; and when the thunder rolls, he thinks the gods are fighting. The little child firmly believes in fairies, and cannot picture a king without his crown. But increase of knowledge comes, with increase of sorrow; voices begin to whisper to the heart, 'Have you not asked them that go by the way?' until at last, in that widening experience, the errors of the savage are detected, and the dreams that were childhood's music are dispelled. It was a very painful progress for poor Job, and it has been very painful, too, for poor humanity. The mightiest task of history has not been to build theories ; the mightiest task of history has been to shatter them. We start with error. We start with misconception. We start with views of God that are all wrong. And only slowly, through the pressure of sorrow, through the struggle of ages, through the death of martyrs, does the race, like this patriarch, reach these roomy thoughts that can be tested and tried by every fact.

Think of this duty in relation to happiness. We have all our dreams of happiness in life's glad morning. We are as certain that we know how to be happy, as Job's three friends were that they knew God's ways. When we win *this*, when we get *that*, we shall be happy. The birds will sing then, and all the day be golden. *Have ye not asked them that go by the way?* They could have told vou that all that the world can give may be poured into your lap to make you happy, and yet in the core of it may be a pain, and a heart that is half in love with easeful death.

They could have told you that 'the mind is its own place and of itself can make a heaven of hell, a hell of heaven.' They could have told you that not to win this or that, but to be faithful, loving, gentle, and sincere, is the one way to what the world's a-seeking.

Think of this duty in relation to moral responsibility. There are many influences at work to-day to lighten that burden of responsibility. We have learned something of the evolution of conscience. We are all glamoured by that magic word heredity. We are not so sure as our forefathers were of the foundations and the record of our faith. May we not, then, take a little liberty? Is sin after all so exceeding sinful? *Have ye not asked them that go by the way?* Let them tell you if conscience has ceased to be a torment. Let them tell you if they have lost nothing by their sin. Let them unfold the story of their lives, at the best tarnished, and at the worst degraded, and you will thank God that at the outset of manhood you brought your theory to the great test of facts.

Think of this duty in relation to religion. I

know what many young folk think about religion. It is all well enough for the old and for the sickly, but they are neither old nor sickly yet, thank God. They are not going to be gloomy and long-faced ; they want more exciting joys than the prayer-meeting. They want their liberty, and to become religious, they think, is to sap the life-blood out of everything. *Have ye not asked them that go by the way?* They could have told you that to be a Christian is freedom, power, manhood, vision, joy. *I* am the way, says the Master whom we serve. The facts are all in favour of Christ Jesus.

THE GLORY AND THE GATE

And Mordecai came again to the king's gate.—Esther vi. 12.

A WORD or two will be sufficient to recall to you this most fascinating and dramatic story. King Ahasuerus, unable to sleep one night, had bidden his attendants read to him. The book he chose was the annals of his kingdom, and the passage on which the reader lighted was a narrative of an attempt on the king's life, which had been baffled by the promptitude of Mordecai. The king had known nothing of the plot; he resolved to reward Mordecai in the morning; so in the morning, summoning in Haman his grand-vizier, Ahasuerus asked him, 'What shall be done unto the man whom the king delighteth to honour?' Now Haman had an overweening conceit of himself, and like other conceited persons, he could be very stupid. Surely the man whom the king wished to honour could be no one else than his own important self? Haman suggested a royal procession through the town, assured that he would be the central figure in it. Then the king told him that the man was Mordecai, and if there was one person in Persia whom Haman hated, that person was none other than Mordecai. And the king bade Haman lead the horse by the bridle, and cry out the praises of Mordecai through the city. It was a very agony of humiliation for Haman ; but the word of the king would brook no contradiction. So Mordecai, clothed in a robe of state, and mounted on a richly caparisoned palfrey from the royal mews, went in procession through the streets of Shushan ; and Haman, at his bridle-rein, kept crying before him, 'Thus shall it be done unto the man whom the king delighteth to honour.'

Now whether Mordecai was a gate-keeper, and had some official post at the palace-door ; or whether he was just a frequenter of that neighbourhood where the Orientals pass so many of their leisure hours, is a question of little moment for my purpose. All I desire you to bear in mind is this, that the king's gate was Mordecai's station. It was here that he was commonly to be found. It was his familiar and ordinary place.

Such business as he had he would transact there. There he would exchange news with his friends. Then suddenly came that hour of exaltation. He became the hero of ten thousand eyes. There was not a square but was crowded with eager citizens, there was not a window nor a housetop but was thronged, as Mordecai moved forward through the city. It was an hour of thrilling and unexampled triumph for an exiled Jew in a barbarian capital. How would it leave him? Would he be changed and spoiled? Would the strong current of his Jewish heart be stemmed? *And Mordecai came again to the king's gate.* Here was his place, here was his daily post. He had not forgotten it in the re-echoing cheers. The king might honour him, and he would accept the honour, but the balance of his life must not be destroyed. Mordecai was conspicuously great— no one will doubt that who reads this little book ; but he was never greater than when, after a day of triumph, he came again to the king's gate.

I trust, then, that you begin to see the thought that underlies our simple text. When you strip away the Oriental trapping, you get to the beating

heart of all humanity.   To every one of us come
hours of unsettlement, as there came this tumultuous day to Mordecai.   Sometimes they leap on
us quite unexpectedly ; sometimes they are the
crown of years of striving.   And how such hours
will leave us when they pass is one of the vital
questions of all life.   Shall we be changed?   Will
the old peace be gone ?   Will the religion that
guided us, and the work that satisfied us ; the
hopes that cheered us, and the friendships that
eased us—will these go by the board in that
tempestuous hour ?   I pray God that it may not
be so.   There is a certain stability of purpose
that is absolutely needful for all moral excellence.
'And Mordecai came again to the king's gate.'

I wish to take that thought suggested by our
text, and to apply it in one or two spheres of our
experience.   And first, I should like to say a word
on holidays.   There are many thousands in this
city to-night who have just returned from a brief
annual holiday.[1]   There is not a glen in Scotland
so remote, and not a village or hamlet so secluded,
but has had some son or daughter home from
Glasgow.   The mills were silent ; shipyards were

---

[1] Preached on the Sunday after the Glasgow Fair Holidays.

strangely still; some of the streets had quite a Sabbath quietude. For multitudes the routine was broken, and the drudgery over for a little time. That hard-won liberty is very sweet, in the warmth of summer-time, and when the days are golden; but I think there are few who are not unsettled by it, when the hour comes for taking up work again. When Mordecai dismounted from his charger, and handed back the gorgeous robes he had worn, I dare say the king's gate looked dustier and drearier than it had seemed before the hour of glory. And life is never more dusty and more dreary, nor is the routine of toil ever more irksome, than after a few days when all the bonds are broken, and when we may wander at our own sweet will. I have known men who would never take a holiday, they felt it so unsettled and upset them. That is a poor way of slipping through life. It was not Mordecai's, and it should not be ours. By every wave that breaks upon the shore, and by every hill on which the sunshine rests, by the reviving of sweet memories of childhood, by the renewing of old and dear and precious ties, God honours us more royally than Mordecai was honoured, and like Mordecai, we should accept it all. Then, not in a fretful or rebellious spirit, but cheerfully and bravely, we should return to our task and to our cross, as Mordecai came to the king's gate.

But there is another sphere where this is equally important. I refer to the trials and sorrows with which we meet. I think that many of you will understand my meaning when I talk of the unsettlement of a great sorrow. A man may live in the sunshine many years, until he almost forgets what trouble is. Day succeeds day in an unbroken happiness, and all the voices in the world are music. Then suddenly, like a bolt out of the blue, comes the dread moment of which we never dreamed. Friendship is broken. There is disgrace at home. Some one we loved with all our heart is dead. Like one of these storms so frequent in the tropics, that with incredible swiftness break from a cloudless sky, tempests have swept on many a heart and home. Such times are times of very strange unsettlement. The world that we moved in seems very far away. It seems incredible that only yesterday we were talking and trafficking like other men. We have lived so intensely and have borne so much, that a year has seemed to pass us in a day.

Now I do not mean even to suggest that one can live through such seasons and emerge unchanged. A stoical philosopher might have done it, but the age of the stoic philosophers is gone. It is told of one of them that when a friend announced to him the death of his only son, he said, 'I never thought I had begotten an immortal.' That was the ideal of manly courage once; it is not the ideal of manly courage now. Whatever else the gospel of Christ has done, it has singularly deepened the affections. Hearts are more tender since Jesus lived and died, affections are deeper, love is ennobled infinitely. And hence the bitterness and sorrow of *our* tragic hours is deeper than any that the pagan knew. How shall we bear it? That is the vital question. How shall we master it, that it do not overwhelm us and leave us in the barren sorrow of despair? I know no other answer than our text: And Mordecai came again to the king's gate. Quietly to resume the interrupted task, faithfully to get back to daily duty, patiently to gather up the threads again, silently to bury much and to be

brave ; it is in that return to common life, and to
the common services that God demands of us,
that the cross and the burden are most wisely
borne. Jesus, having been tempted in the wilderness, went back to Galilee to teach and heal.
Peter and John, being released from prison, did
not fly abroad : they went to their own company.
Mordecai came again to the king's gate.

There is an oft-quoted passage in a speech by
that most pure and single-hearted statesman, John
Bright. It refers to the period when Bright
had lost his young wife, and was plunged into
the depths of sorrow. His life seemed to be
shattered at his feet, hope had departed, all his
ambition was dead; and it was then that Cobden
came to see him. And Cobden might have
merely wept with him, and even that would have
been sympathy. Or Cobden might have proposed
a trip through Europe, and that, too, would have
been very kindly. But Cobden did a great deal
better than that. He said, 'Bright, when the
first paroxysm of grief is over, we shall think of
the wives and the children throughout England,
and we shall go out and speak for them, and we
shall go out and fight for them, and we shall

never rest till the corn-laws are repealed.' It was a summons to service, a call to action ; and the gallant heart began to beat again. It may be that all suffering is honour. It may be that when a man is decked in woe, invisible forms precede him through the streets, crying to all who have the ears to hear : ' Thus shall it be done to the man whom the King delighteth to honour.' That may be so. It is not for me to say. God wraps His blessings up in strange disguises. But whether or no, you will not forget now, that Mordecai came again to the king's gate.

Then, lastly, I want to take our text and use it in reference to the spiritual life.

It was a great honour that was done to Mordecai. It was peculiarly consonant to Eastern ideas of splendour. There was a picturesqueness in it, and a wealth of colour, that were very dear to the Oriental heart. There are thousands of men and women in the East to-night, to whom this dramatic and barbaric splendour is still the epitome of exaltation. They would think that their cup was running over, if shah or sultan honoured them like that. Yet what a cheap and childish honouring it was, matched with the favour

of our King of kings ! The heart that is crowned
with the glory of the gospel is a thousand times
more honoured than Mordecai. His was an
outward glory, ours is an inward ; it is the
illumination of heart and will and conscience.
His was a passing glory, ours is a permanent ;
for neither height nor depth, nor life nor death,
shall separate us from the love of Christ. *Thus*
shall it be done unto the man whom the King
delighteth to honour : he shall be called out of
bondage into spiritual liberty ; he shall be clad
in the garments of recreated manhood ; he shall
find life and love and duty rich in meaning ; he
shall move heavenward amid a cloud of witnesses.
The honour of Mordecai was remarkable, but the
honour of the humblest Christian far surpasses it.

Have you received that honour from the
King ? Then this shall be my closing word to
you. Welcome it joyfully, as Mordecai did, and
then get back to the king's gate again. It were
a great thing to be a mighty preacher, and to have
thousands swaying at your word. It were a noble
service to become a missionary, and preach the
gospel of Christ in darkest Africa. But if God
has got work like that in store for you, there will

be no mistaking the summons when it comes. Meantime there is the round of common duty ; there is the daily burden, the ordinary life. Bring the new heart to bear upon all that, if you really want to copy Mordecai. Be a better mother among your growing children. Be a more thoughtful husband ; be a sweeter wife. Be a more considerate daughter in the home. Be a more chivalrous brother to your sisters. It takes the grace of God to do the least thing graciously, and the grace of God is given us for that. If there is any one here who has heard the call of God to go and serve in the forefront of the battle : then go, break every tie, be not disobedient to the heavenly vision ! But as for the rest of you—will you remember that Mordecai came again to the king's gate ?

A SOUL TO LET

When the unclean spirit is gone out of a man, he walketh through dry places, seeking rest, and findeth none.

Then he saith, I will return into my house from whence I came out; and when he is come, he findeth it empty, swept, and garnished.
—Matt. xii. 43-4.

Our Lord had a quick eye for moral tragedies, and in the pictorial setting of these two verses He has delineated one of the saddest of them all. One marvels at the sure touch of Christ in dealing with the disasters of the soul. Men felt instinctively that He would understand them, and so they came to Him when things were going wrong. And one of the inexplicable wonders about Jesus is this sure insight into secret failures. When we have failed, we grasp a brother's failure, our insight is the child of fellow-feeling. There are whole ranks of tragedies we never suspect, just because God has mercifully guarded us from them. But Christ, in the panoply of perfect manhood, was separated from every taint of sin, and yet had an exquisite understanding of the sinner. It is something, my brother, to feel that you are known. Your tragedy is not so secret as you thought. You are haunted with a dull sense to-night, that unless there is effort and clearing of your feet, your last state is going to be worse than your first; and Christ has spoken on that theme long ago.

Now what strikes us first in this man with an unclean spirit is, that all his tragedy was underground. I mean by that that his very nearest and dearest never suspected what had been going on. If you had asked some villager about him, he would have answered, 'He is an unclean beast.' And if ten years later you had asked again, you would have been told he had been going downhill steadily. Steadily, gradually, so it had seemed to everybody. Always a little worse, a little lower. And only Christ knew that that view was false—the man had been standing at the gates of freedom once! He had played the man against his tyrannous vices. He had cast them out, and cried to God to help him. He had breathed liberty, and tasted the joy of triumph, and known what a noble thing it was to live! And when the ousted tenants came back again, and the old disorder began to reign within, none knew but Christ the struggle, the cry, the passion to be free, of the man whom all the village thought a prisoner.

Are not many of our tragedies underground? They are transacted in the hidden sphere. There are molten fires under the vines of Etna. There are hidden graves among the garden-flowers. And we sow and water the flowers in our garden, just to conceal the sepulchre that is there. Who knows how you have dreamed, how you have struggled?—and men look at you and call you contented, merry! But there are memories of prayer stored in your heart, and of days when your life seemed utterly unworthy, and you stood up and cast the devils out. And they are all back again to-night, and never a soul in this city knows of it, except yourself and Christ.

But there is another feature in this story besides its secrecy. It is the story of an unused triumph. This man did not fail because he never won; there was one morning when his heart was clean. That was his day of victory, and the promise of final conquest was in that, but he misused

his victory and was lost.   One of the saddest
stories ever written is just the story of our mis-
managed triumphs.   It is our little victories that
curse us, because we have neither head nor heart
to manage them.   We are so apt to be self-centred
in success ; so ready to forget how weak we are ;
so prone to think that the campaign is ours,
because in one skirmish the enemy has fled.   Then
we grow careless, we do not walk with God ;
we do not garrison our heart against assault ; and
in an hour when we think not comes the old
temptation, strong, subtle, doubly sweet because
forsworn, and we are taken unawares and mastered,
and our last state is worse than our first.

I have often thought, on reading this little
parable, of the wonderful wisdom of Jesus in *His*
victory.   I have often thought of the self-restraint
of Christ, when He triumphed over sin and over
death.   If there was ever a triumph in the history
of earth used for the lasting blessing of mankind,
it was the triumph of Jesus when He rose.
There was a sweet restraint in resurrection joy.
There was no spectacle of a risen Saviour for the
crowd.   There was a watchful reserve, a choosing
of times and companies, a holy management of

the resurrection glory, that mark the risen Saviour as divine. Even Christ was guarded in His hour of triumph—how much more guarded should the Christian be ? This man cast out the unclean spirit, and said all 's well. And his last state was worse than his first !

And you see what his peculiar danger was? It was the peril of the empty heart. His soul lay vacant, that was the pity of it. There was room for the ousted devil to return. Some men are tempted because their hearts are full. Life is so rich, so strong in a thousand interests, there is no room in it for Christ at all. But many are tempted because their hearts are empty, and the old ways creep back again to stay. It is not sufficient to expel the wrong. We must fill the emptied heart with nobler things. A tenantless heart—a soul that is to let—is a standing invitation to the devil.

It was there the man of our story failed. Have you never failed just at that point ? There was struggle with evil, and momentary triumph, there was an empty and swept and garnished house. And that was something ; you were right proud of it, after the moral disorder of the past.

But you forgot that a habit expelled is not by any means a habit slain. You forgot that new interests must fill the life if the old interests are never to lodge again. It was because no ruling passion had been begotten, that you began to hanker for the old again. It was because there was no new enthusiasm, no worthier tenants to occupy the soul, that you craved for the ousted things and drew them back. Had the empty house been filled with a new purpose, controlled by a new hand and nobler will, the cast-out spirit would have acknowledged defeat, and felt there was no room in that soul for him. It was the soul to let that did the harm.

And so I bring you face to face with the great mystery of an indwelling Christ. I want you to set that truth in the light of all I have been saying, until you see how practical it is. These deepest doctrines of the word of God were never meant to be speculative wonders—it is when we live them, we find how real they are—and it is Christ in you the hope of glory, that saves you from the peril of the empty heart. The gospel does not merely come to you and say, 'My brother, my sister, you must give up that sin.' It does not

bid you empty your heart of evil, and leave it
empty and garnished to the end. It knows the
danger of a soul unoccupied ; the certain fall of a
heart without a tenant. And so the gospel is
prepared to give you something far better than
what it drives away. It is prepared to inhabit
the temple of your heart with the Holy Spirit
of the Lord Jesus Christ. Know ye not that
your bodies are temples of the Holy Ghost who
dwelleth in you? That is the glad exchange
the gospel makes. In place of the unclean spirit
who is gone, the spirit of the Lord comes in to
dwell.

Now where the spirit of the Lord is, there is
liberty, and where the spirit of the Lord is, there
is life. And it is that new liberty and life within
the heart that make us strong when old things
steal back again. 'I can do all things,' cried
the apostle—not through a barred door and an
empty heart—'I can do all things through Christ
which strengtheneth me'; his empty and swept
and garnished heart was full. O brother, you
have been fighting out your sin. But what you
want is a new enthusiasm in its place. And I
wish to ask you seriously and simply, have you

ever made room for Him to take Him in ? There
is love, there is power, there is liberty in Christ.
Open your heart. Receive the gift of God. It
is in the bitter hour of temptation that men find
the worth of an indwelling Saviour.

For our old sins are hungering to get back.
That truth is clearly written in our text. They
are houseless and homeless, and restless and ill at
ease. They crave their old shelter in our lives
again. And you do not mean to give it to them.
No ! you are done with the past for ever and a
day. But so was the hero of our text to-night, and
yet his last state was to be lost. Your cast-off
vices are not dead. They are going to return in
subtle ways. Do not pride yourself on a swept and
garnished house ; there is no pledge of victory
in that. But there *is* in a heart where dwells the
love of Christ, and something of the high power
of His passion. It is in Him that we are more
than conquerors. It is in Him that our last state
shall be our best.

'Oh ! come to my heart, Lord Jesus,
There is room in my heart for Thee.'

THE IRKSOMENESS OF RELIGION

There is nothing at all, beside this manna, before our eyes.—
Numb. xi. 6.

WE all know how after a certain time the children of Israel began to loathe the manna. They remembered the rich produce of their Egyptian gardens, and began, in the desert, to crave for it again. The manna tasted like fresh oil, we are told, and in another passage we read that it was like honey. Be sure it was wholesome, and quite sufficiently palatable, if it came from God for the sustenance of His children. He was their Father, and when they asked for bread, you may be certain they would not get a stone. Yet for all that, Israel despised the manna. Their soul rejected it, it was light food. It was bread from heaven, says the psalmist—angels' bread— and yet it proved distasteful to the camp.

Now had it proved distasteful to their enemies, I think I could have understood it better. God

did not give it to support His enemies, He gave
it for the sustaining of His children. Had some
Amalekite boy stolen out at sunrise, when the
dew lay heavy, and the manna on the dew, and
had he gathered a handful of the substance,
tempted to do it by the Israelite children—had
some Amalekite boy done that, then tasted it,
and found it exceedingly unpleasant and bitter, I
could have taken that as the punishment of God
on him for laying his hands on covenanted mercies.
But the Israelites were a covenanted people—out
of Egypt have I called My son. They were being
led about by the Almighty ; they were on God's
highway to the land of promise. The strange
thing is that it was they—and not God's enemies
—who found the manna such a distasteful dish.
It was the children of Israel who felt the diet
irksome, and the children of Israel were the
people of God.

Now that leads me by quite a competent
spiritualising—for did not Jesus say 'I am the
bread'?—to dwell on a very urgent matter, I mean
the irksomeness inherent in religion. I am not
talking of hypocrites to-night. I am handling
something far more delicate than the accepted

irksomeness of all hypocrisy. And I am not talking of the ungodly, nor of the men who have conceived false views about religion, nor of the women who have been led to think of religion as something other than it really is. All these must picture religion as an irksome thing, and it is perfectly natural that they should. But I am talking of God's professing people, as the children of Israel were out in the wilderness. I am speaking to those who have really been called out of Egypt, and are honestly struggling heavenwards through the desert. And I want to touch upon this strange, sad fact, that to them religion should often be an irksome thing.

Now at first glance, and from an external standpoint, it might seem impossible that it should be so. For to begin with (some one might say to me), if religion is anything at all, it must be the greatest concern in human life, and if anything be that, it cannot be irksome. Yes, religion is the chief concern in life. There is no relationship of man to man, there is no relationship of man to society—there is nothing on earth so paramount and vital as the relationship of the human soul to God. Yet men who have felt all that, and feel it now—and wherever an awakened soul is, there it is felt—such men and women, whensoever they reveal their souls, confess to the seasons, sometimes unbroken years, when religion was an irksome thing to them.

Or again, one might say religion cannot be irksome if the great key-words of the New Testament be true. If there is any meaning in these recurring notes that make the peculiar music of the gospel, it is surely impossible that it be irksome. What are these key-words? One of them is rest. Can there ever be any irksomeness in rest? And another is joy—the gospel rings with joy. Can real joy ever grow distasteful? And love, that is another gospel note; and strength, and victory, and satisfaction. If these be the gains and the heritage of Christians, how can religion be an irksome thing? Now all these *are* the Christian's, certainly. There is rest, and there is joy and love on the narrow path which Jesus Christ hath trodden. But for all that, there are few travellers on that path who have not felt the irksomeness of their religion.

We detect it sometimes by the quiet relief we

feel when our religious exercises are concluded—
a certain secret sense of satisfaction when the
prayer is got over, and the worship done. Not
that we were not in earnest when we prayed; we
gave our heart to it, it was no empty form. Still
it required an effort to make us pray, we had to
drag ourselves by sheer will-power to the throne,
and however truly and heartily we pled with God
and laid our case before Him in petition, when
the prayer was over we felt a kind of freedom,
as if a hard duty were honourably done. Now
prayer is the very climax of religion. It is the
soul at last in communion with its God. And if
we loved God with all our heart and soul, it
ought to be an exquisite joy to speak to Him.
Yet it is not always that—perhaps seldom so.
Read the biography of any saint. It took a
certain determination and doggedness, a quiet
mastery of impulse and desire, to preserve alive
the habit of devotion. And all that is a proof
that in the serious life there is something irksome
even to the saint.

We detect it again in the way in which many
try to put service in the place of personal religion.
I thank God for all the loyal service that is being

lavished on His church to-day. The body of
Christ is only beginning to realise that it has
come not to be ministered unto but to minister.
It is a lofty and a true conception, and it is
kindling the church into undreamed-of energy.
But when we see—and if we have eyes we see it
—how many noble men and loyal women are not
keeping the balance of the religious life, but
gradually, perhaps unconsciously, are giving less
thought to personal religion and more and more
to the service of their church—I say they are
yielding to one of the subtlest temptations of the
age, laying a false accent on the outward, and by
yielding to the echoing cry for work, shunning
the irksomeness of personal piety. But to shun
it—what is that but to confess it? To acknowledge that though they trust they are Christ's,
there is somewhat distasteful in the inward life?
And then to make up, as it were, for the lack
of soul-religion, they become doubly feverish in
outward work.

But the irksomeness of a quiet and abiding
piety is seen above all in the love of religious
excitement. Excitement and novelty in religious
things could have no charm at all for any man, if

he were truly in love with personal religion, and
eager above all for a closer walk with God.
When a man is in love with his own quiet fire-
side, he can scarcely be tempted to go abroad of
an evening. In the gracious peace of his sweet if
humble home, and in his intercourse with the
glorious dead through books, he would as soon
think of going to the Pole as to the shallow
excitement of a third-rate theatre. Indeed,
when a man is always hurrying there, and hither
and thither to every showy function, we may be
sure that there is not much—what shall I call it ?—
not much heart-satisfaction by his hearth. And
as with the home, so is it with the soul. It is
ill at ease at home, and wants variety. And
all the love of excitement and of novelty,
and the foolish running to any new attrac-
tion, and the extraordinary sale of childish
books ; all this, with the growing demand for
sensational preaching—against which every true
preacher will set his face like a flint—is a token
of how irksome a thing deep, silent piety is.
If it were not so irksome, there would be no
call for novelty.

Now I wonder if we can discern the grounds

of this element of irksomeness in heart-religion?
Surely the first and the deepest is just this—
religion is spiritual, and we are carnal. At the
very best, we are but bruised reeds ; at our
noblest, we are but smoking flax. And religion,
in the full compass of her powers, has her dwelling 'above the smoke and stir of this dim spot.'
She handles the things invisible and eternal, she
draws her warrants from remote transactions ;
she speaks of powers we cannot trace or measure,
she looks with a queenly scorn on sense and
time. And we are such creatures of the seen
and tangible, groping and clambering into the
clearer air with such infinite effort and recurrent
failure that the unchanging calm of the ideal of
holiness strikes on us ofttimes as a barbed thing.
What is religion but to walk with God?
And for impurity to walk with purity, and sin
with holiness, and flesh with spirit—the elements
of an irksome journey are all there. It is
because we are far from Christlike yet ; it is
because God is holiness and love and purity
and truth, and because in religion we must
walk with God, that even to the saint it has its
irksomeness.

Another reason for that same feeling is this, we strive and seem to make so little progress. We do not advance, as an army does to battle. We often seem just to be marking time. There are no habits, I believe, which hold us so lightly as the habits of piety and of devotion. There are none that snap more easily than they—and the old life is back with us again. A man may have prayed in secret through a winter, yet when summer comes the habit drops away. Or he may long have read his Bible and attended worship, but when some change of circumstances overtakes him, how quickly he forgets his honoured custom! It is all this haunting sense of unreality, this lack of steady progress to a goal; it is the fact that with every morning as it comes we have just to begin the whole thing over again—it is this, a kind of want of continuity, that to the saintliest may make religion irksome.

But in our religion, I think it is the *Cross* above all else that does it. It is the fact that in the very centre there hangs the pallid figure on the tree. In every mood and in every duty of the Christian there lies the shadow of the cross of

Christ. What is discipleship?—take up thy cross and bear it. And who is worthy to be the follower of Jesus?—only he who bears his cross. And to men and women such as we are, cross-bearing will be irksome to the end. In other words, it is the abnegation, it is the humility and self-denial, it is the renunciation of much that is sweet to us, and the eye fixed on a dying and bleeding Saviour ; it is *that*, when life is sweet and full of music, and calling us as to the freedom of a bird, that may keep an element of irksomeness in all following of the blessed Lord.

Now I have been preaching to myself to-night. I have been writing down, for my own help and comfort, my thoughts on a subject that have much troubled me. You may have never felt religion irksome. God has been very good to you ; praise Him for it. But if you *have* felt it, and if you feel it now, do not say you are not His, and do not charge yourself with being a hypocrite, and above all do not give in. What you are feeling, the saints of God have felt. They too, like you, have ' wrestled on towards heaven '*gainst* storm and wind and tide.' And be sure that when you

lay aside this body, and at the touch of death—
most kind and timely—the preparation for eternity
is done, be sure that then, in the presence and
love of God, all irksomeness will be gone for
evermore.

THE PRE-REQUISITE OF VISION

When they were awake, they saw His glory.—Luke ix. 32.

I⊤ is very strange to find the disciples heavy with
sleep, even on the Mount of Transfiguration.
One would have thought that there, if anywhere,
there were things happening that would have
'murdered sleep.' The glory of heaven was
shining forth from Jesus, like sunshine pouring
itself irresistibly through cloud; there too, not in
any ghostly apparition, but in most strange reality,
were men who had been dead for centuries; yet
in the presence of such scenes as these, Peter and
James and John were very sleepy. Then they
awoke, startled we know not how. Gradually, as
a swimmer might rise to the surface out of deep
waters, they came to themselves, and remembered
where they were. And then, and not till then,
when they were fully awake, the gospel tells us
that they saw His glory.

You see, then, that one of the penalties of living

sleepily, is that we miss so much of what is happening. The mightiest transactions may be forward, and heaven be stooping down to touch the mountain-tops, but we shall see nothing of it all if we be drowsy. The latest biographer of Principal Cairns, in his most satisfactory and illuminative little volume, gives us a very charming account of Cairns's schooldays. He tells us that very early in the morning, when the house was still, Cairns was already busy with his books. His brothers were fast asleep, so was his father ; no one was stirring in the cottage save his mother. She was already hard at work in her day's toils, not grudgingly, but perhaps singing as she worked. Now Cairns had a limitless admiration for his mother ; she was his heroine and his saint right to the end. And his biographer suggests that this love and adoration might be traced, in part, to these early morning hours. The cottage was radiant with love and toil and sacrifice. But the others were heavy with sleep, and did not see it. None but the zealous young student were awake ; but when he was awake, he saw her glory.

Now it is one mark of every great awakening

that it reveals to us unexpected glories. When
intellect is quickened and the feelings are moved ;
when the will is reinforced and conscience
purified, the world immediately ceases to be
commonplace, and clothes itself in unsuspected
splendour. You might play the noblest music to
a savage, and it would carry little meaning to his
ear. You might set him down before some
magnificent painting, and it would not stir one
chord in all his being. But when a man has
breathed the spirit of the West, and been enriched
by its heritage of feeling, there are thoughts that
wander off into eternity in every masterpiece of
art—we have been wakened, and we see the
glory. Do you think it is an idle figure of
speech when we talk of the long sleep of the
Middle Ages? Do you imagine that we are only
using metaphor when we describe the Reformation as an awakening? I hardly think that we
could speak more literally than when we use such
simple terms as these. There is always a world
of glorious environment; but men were heavy
with sleep once, and they missed it. It was not
till powers and faculties were quickened in the
great movements of Renaissance and Reform, that

the clouds scattered and the blue heaven was seen. And if to-day there is larger meaning in our life, if nature is richer in spiritual significance, if faith and hope and love are far more worthy, if religion is deeper and God more real and tender ; it can all be interpreted in the language of the text : When they were fully awake, they saw the glory.

I think, too, that in spiritual awakening we find that the suggestion of our text arrests us. There are many glories which we never see, till the call of our Lord has bidden us awake. There is the Bible, for instance ; think of that a moment. We have been taught out of its pages since we were little children, and we can never be grateful enough for this so priceless book, that is alive with interest even to the child. It is the noblest of all noble literature. It is fearless, and frank, and eloquent, and simple. It faces life's depths, yet it is always hopeful. It fronts life's tragedies, yet it is always calm. A man may refuse to believe it is inspired, yet may acknowledge what a debt he owes it. But it is one thing to feel the Bible's charm, and it is another thing to see the Bible's glory ; and the glory of the

Bible is a hidden glory, until a man is spiritually awake. It is only then that it speaks as friend with friend, and that it separates itself from common voices. It is only then that it reaches us apart, with a message and a music no one else shall hear. It is only then, under the pressure of sorrow, or in the darkness of failure, or beneath the shadow of warring duties, that it touches us as if we were alone in the whole world. That is the glory of love, and of love's literature. And we know much before we wake, but never *that*. It is as true of us as of the three upon the mountain—when they were fully awake, they saw the glory.

Or think again of the life of our brother man. Until we are awakened by the gospel, I question if we ever see the full glory there. To most of us the life of thousands of our fellows seems a most dull and commonplace affair. There is little radiance in it, and little hope ; it is as cheerless as a grey sea in late November. But can imagination not do anything ? Certainly, imagination can work wonders. If you want to see the charm of common lives ; the passion, the tenderness, the joy, the strength of the persons whom you and I

would brush past heedlessly, just read the *Bleak
House* of Charles Dickens again.

> 'The poem hangs on the berry-bush
> Till comes the poet's eye;
> And the whole street is a masquerade
> When Shakespeare passes by.'

All that is true. And all that should make us
very grateful to God for the gift of every real
novelist and dramatist. But underneath all life
of passion and affection there are spiritual possibilities for the meanest, and not till the world
is wakened by the gospel are the hidden
glories of humanity revealed. Why are we
carrying on home-mission work? Is it merely
to employ our leisure energies? It is because
we have been wakened, and have seen the glory
of the poorest brother in the meanest street.
And why have we missionaries in India and in
Africa? Is it because we fear the heathen will
be damned for not having trusted One of whom
they never heard? It is because we have
been wakened, and have seen the glory of every
heart that beats in darkest Africa. Under all
vice there is still something true; deeper than
the deepest degradation, there is still a hope

unspeakable and full of glory ; in the barren
desert the rose may blossom yet, and Jesus Christ
has wakened us to that. There was the ring of
the true faith about Chalmers of New Guinea
when, writing of a cannibal chief of that dark
island, he refers to him as 'that grand old
gentleman.'

And the same thing is true of our dear Lord
Himself. We must be spiritually wakened if we
would see His glory. It is only then that He
reveals Himself, in the full and glorious compass
of His grace. When a man approaches Christ
Jesus intellectually, he is humbled and stirred by
that wealth of spontaneous wisdom. And when
a man approaches Christ emotionally, the sympathy of that matchless heart may overpower
him. But the brightest intellect and the most
delicate emotions may centre themselves for a
lifetime on the Saviour, yet the glory of the
Saviour may escape them ; it is always difficult
for the man who is spiritually dead to understand
the dominion of Christ in history. But the hour
comes when a man is spiritually roused. Out of
the infinite, the hand of God hath touched him.
The old content is gone like some sweet dream.

He realises that things seen are temporal. He
is not satisfied any more, nor very happy ; sin
becomes real, the eternal is full of voices. And
it is then, in a vision fairer than any dawn, that
the glory of Christ first breaks upon the soul.
There is a depth of meaning in His wisdom
now, that the mere intellect was powerless to
grasp. There is a tenderness and a strength in
His compassion that mere emotion never understood. There is a value and a nearness in His
death that once would have been quite inexplicable. When they were awake, they saw His
glory.

But to pass on from that great theme of
spiritual wakening, there is one feature of experience which I must not omit. It is part of God's
discipline with us in the years, that the years
should waken us to see glories which once we
missed. The value of our college education is
not the amount of raw knowledge which it gives
us. There are men whose minds are amazingly
full of facts, yet no one would call them educated
men. And there are others who have compara-
tively few facts at their command, yet you instinctively recognise that they are educated. For true

education is not meant to store us ; true education
is intended to awaken us; and the joy of the
truly educated man is no poor pride in his
superior knowledge : it is that he has been so
wakened that in every realm and sphere he can
see glories unobserved before.

Now if this be true of our schools and of our
colleges, do you not think it holds also of God's
education ?   It is a truth we should ever keep
clear before us.   There are mysteries in life's
discipline we cannot fathom ; there are strange
happenings that have baffled every thinker ; but
at least we know that the change and the stress
of years, and the joys they bring with them, and
their losses and gains, waken us, perhaps rudely,
out of many a dream, and show us glories which
once we never saw.   I do not think that the man
who has never been poor will be quick to see
the heroisms of quiet poverty.   I do not think
that he who is always strong can ever appreciate
at its full moral value the dauntless cheerfulness
of the racked invalid.   You must have been
tempted as your brother is, to know his magnificent courage in resisting.   To the man who
never loved, love is inscrutable.   So the Almighty,

in whose hands we are, disciplines us through the deepening of the years, wakes us by change, by love, by sorrow, by temptation, until the veils are rent that shrouded other hearts. And we say of humanity what these three said of Jesus : 'When we were awake, we saw His glory.'

But the deepest interpretation of the text is not of this world. It will come to its crown of meaning in eternity. It is then that out of the sleep of life we shall awaken, and we shall be satisfied when we awake. We shall see the glory of goodness and of truth then, as we never saw it in our brightest hours. We shall see the glory of having kept on struggling, when every voice was bidding us give in. We shall see the glory of the love we once despised, of insignificant and unrewarded lives, of the silence that shielded and the speech that cheered. We shall see the glory of Jesus and of God. We are heavy with sleep here, even at our best. It is going to take the touch of death to waken us. But when we waken in the eternal morning, I think we shall truly see the glory then.

THE NOTE OF THE HEROIC

His eyes were as a flame of fire.—Rev. i. 14.

It is notable that in this vision of the ascended
Saviour, the eyes should have been as it were a
flame of fire. That is hardly the characteristic
we should have expected after hearing of hair
that was as white as snow. The snow-white hair
suggests to us venerable age; it hints at the
passing of unnumbered years, with the inevitable
quenching of the fire of youth; but when we
should look for eyes that were very gentle, or
that were filled with the wise tenderness of age,
we find that His eyes were as a flame of fire.
Now that contrast at once suggests to me this
thought. In Christ there is not only a beauty as
of silvered age; there is also a fire and a heroism
as of youth. And it is on that note of the heroic
that I wish to speak to-night.

I ask you, as we begin to think upon the

matter, to bear in mind one very simple distinction. It is that the thoughts that cluster round the *heroic* are not exactly those which the word *hero* suggests. A hero is just the embodiment of our ideal. He is the man who represents to us all that we dream of, whom we can clothe in every virtue and grace we reckon fine. There is nothing fixed or defined, then, in the meaning of hero; its import is relative to the qualities we admire. The hero of an unscrupulous man of business is often a man who is only more unscrupulous. The heroine of the woman of the world is sometimes only a more worldly woman. In a hero there may be absolutely nothing heroic ; if we are degraded, so shall our ideals be. But heroism is always lofty and disinterested; it is courage touched into self-forgetfulness ; it is enthusiasm with the crown of sacrifice upon its brow ; it is the genius of the heart defying prudence. A hero may have very evil eyes ; but wherever the true heroic is, there the eyes are as a flame of fire.

Now as civilisation advances and grows more complex, there is one kind of heroism that is less and less demanded. It is the heroism that may be described as physical, and that has for its basis what we call animal courage. In a rough and lawless and unsettled time, it might benefit a man little to be gentle. The man who would live must have a ready sword, and wield it valiantly, sometimes, for wife and children. Such times, then, in a nation's history—and we have had long periods like that in Scotland—are times that call out and develop physical heroism. It is always an early epoch in a country that is known by the name of its heroic age. But as civilisation advances, life takes other aspects. The relations of man to man become more intricate. The sword that once was carried in the belt is handed over to be wielded by the law ; life becomes ordered, settled, and secure. There is consummate need to be intelligent and tactful ; there is less need now than once for physical heroism. We are never wakened of a morning now to hear that the Highlands are ' out,' and are marching on the city. And that implies that as civilisation grows, and intercourse increases, and law becomes supreme—and may I add as anæsthetics like chloroform are discovered, that remove the necessity of facing up to pain—the accent is shifted from merely *physical* heroism, and is inevitably placed on other virtues.

But as the need of physical heroism declines, the need of spiritual heroism steadily grows. The very causes that have lessened the value of the one have helped to heighten the value of the other. We are in no danger now from Highland caterans : the dangers that menace us are far more subtle. They spring from that lowering of moral standards that is unavoidable in our complex intercourse. It is not easy to be oneself now, we are so interlocked in what we call society. We have lost a little liberty, with all our gains, and are moulded more into a common pattern. The pressure of public opinion is tremendous, and public opinion makes for an average type. It is, therefore, more difficult now to be honestly true to oneself. It takes a little more heroism than it did once. We are more tempted to conform to common standards, to barter our birthright of individuality, to be what a hundred interests would have us be, rather than the men God meant that we should be. And so the need of spiritual heroism grows, as the need of physical heroism lessens. The hair of His head was white as snow, we read—that does not even suggest a young society. When time has mellowed the spirit of a people, when age has tempered the passion of its youth, when the riot of its blood is somewhat cooled, and it is venerable, stately, and august, it is *then* (if Jesus Christ be living) that there will be eyes that are like a flame of fire.

Now we cannot turn to the earthly life of Jesus without being struck with one marvellous union there. I refer to the union of what was beautiful and gracious, with all that was in the truest sense heroic. We know that a bruised reed He would not break. We cannot fathom the depths of His compassion. There was never a patience like His patience with the twelve; there was never a pity like His pity of the sinner. He was gentle, charitable, courteous, kind, a perfect pattern of moral beauty. But the wonder of that beauty is magnified a hundredfold, when we remember the heroism with which it went hand in hand. If to be true to one's mission and to stand alone; if to be faithful, and joyful, and quiet, and undaunted; if to challenge all the powers of hell to combat; if to march forward

without a falter to a cross—if that be heroism
in its noblest meaning, then Jesus of Nazareth
must have been heroic. Tenderness is great
and heroism is sublime. In Christ there
was tenderness infinite, and heroism matchless.
The eyes that wept beside the grave of
Lazarus were eyes that were like a flame of
fire.

In some degree, then, as we grow like to
Christ, that union of qualities will be found in
us. It is one distinctive mark of that new
character that has been built up through the
powers of the gospel, that there is ample room
in it for all that is gracious, and at the same
time for all that is heroic. There were two great
schools of philosophy in Rome in the age pre-
ceding the entrance of the gospel there. The
one was Stoicism and the other Epicureanism,
and each had its own ideal of human character.
The aim of the Stoic was to foster heroism ; he
crushed out the affections ruthlessly. The aim
of the Epicurean was not heroism, it was just
to fashion amiable gentlemen. But the *needs* of
the human heart broke down the first, for pity
and love demanded recognition. And the

grandeur of the human heart broke down the second, for there is that within each of us that craves for self-sacrifice.   What the world needed was a type of character that could embrace and glorify the two ideals, and I humbly submit that the gospel gave us that.   There is a place in it for pity, there is room for love ; there is dew and sunshine for the tenderest affections that nestle in the shadow of the heart ; but there is room for the heroic too.   We have a cross to carry ; we have a witness to bear.   We have a life to live ; we have a death to die.   We are following a hope that is sublime, and we fare ill without a little heroism.   We shall be poor disciples of a compassionate Lord, unless we have eyes that can soften into pity.   But we shall be poor soldiers in the warfare mystical, unless these eyes are as a flame of fire.

It is notable, too, that as the spiritual life of Christendom has deepened, as it has grown richer with the passing of the ages, it has brought with it a deeper and truer conception of what spiritual heroism really is.   There is a well-known poem by Tennyson under the title of St. Simeon Stylites. It is a gruesome description of one of these pillar-

saints whom people venerated in the Middle Ages.
St. Simeon spends his years on the top of a high
pillar ; he is scorched by the sun and is swept by
the storms of winter. He grows blind and deaf;
he is racked with intolerable agues. He is praying
night and morning for Heaven's pardon. And
round the base of the pillar people are ever
thronging to do reverence to this ascetic saint.
Now that is an extreme case, I grant you willingly ;
and it is almost repulsive, even in Tennyson's
hands. But the fact remains that, in the Middle
Ages, it was such lives that were the types of
moral heroism. Even St. Francis, the gentlest
of all mystics, was desperately cruel to himself.
It was very noble—I think we all feel that. It
was very noble ; but it was mistaken. And we
should thank God that we are living in a time
when the heroism of self-suppression is disowned,
to make room for the nobler heroism of service.
It is not on the tops of pillars that we look for
saints now. It is not in cell or monastery that
we search for heroism. I speak as a Protestant,
for the spiritual types of Roman Catholicism are
still very largely mediæval. The Christian doctor
who in a London hospital sucked out the diph-

theric poison from a poor child's throat; the Christian student who will hold fast to truth, though a score of voices denounce him as heretical; the Christian worker who goes down into the slums and toils there, when all the novelty is gone, for the poor and the fallen for whom Jesus died; the Christian girl, trained in a gentle home, who volunteers for mission-work in Calabar— it is these that are *our* types of the heroic. The heroism of the hermitage is gone. We have drunk more fully of Christ Jesus now. We have seen more deeply into these wonderful eyes, which John says were like a flame of fire.

But I must close, and I do so with two remarks. The first is that there is always danger for a church when the note of the heroic passes from its life. It is very pleasant to be very comfortable, and to talk about one's good-natured congregation. But the eyes of the vision were not good-natured eyes; they were eyes that burned as with a flame of fire. It was heroism that made Christ's kirk in Scotland. And it was heroism that saved Christ's kirk in Scotland. It was secession, and deposition, and disruption,

in the times that are well described as moderate.
And when that uncalculating enthusiasm passes
and leaves us comfortable and statistical, let
us beware lest a voice say to us also, 'I
know thy works, that thou art neither cold
nor hot.'

And the second is : I appeal to the young men
on the ground of the heroism of Christ Jesus.
Mr. FitzGerald, the translator of Omar Khayyám,
in an exquisite little piece he calls 'Euphranor,'
has some suggestive words on chivalry. He says
that the charm of chivalry was just its note of
heroism ; and if it appealed—as it certainly did
appeal—to the bravest and noblest and most
gallant men, it was just because it put the accent
there. May I not do the same with Jesus Christ?
I think it is a true appeal to opening manhood.
Never forget the heroism of Jesus, nor the heroic
in the Christian calling. The time will come
when you will need Christ's tenderness. You
will want a gentle Lord, and you will find Him.
But to-day it is a call to the heroic that appeals,
and I thank God I can hear that call in Christ.
Go ! mother, bowed with a mother's sorrow—go
to the graveside where Jesus wept. But eager,

gallant, generous heart of youth—why should I lead *you* to that scene of tears? You crave a heroic captain for the battle, and the eyes of Christ are as a flame of fire.